FM 4-90 (FM 4-90.7)

BRIGADE SUPPORT BATTALION

August 2010

DISTRIBUTION RESTRICTION: Approved for public release; distribution is unlimited.

Headquarters, Department of the Army

Published by Books Express Publishing
Books Express Publishing, 2011
ISBN 978-1-78039-944-7

Books Express publications are available from all good retail and online booksellers. For publishing proposals and direct ordering please contact us at: info@books-express.com

***FM 4-90** (FM 4-90.7)

Field Manual
No. 4-90

Headquarters
Department of the Army
Washington, DC, 31 August 2010

Brigade Support Battalion

Contents

DISTRIBUTION RESTRICTION: Approved for public release; distribution is unlimited.

This publication supersedes FM 4-90.7, dated 10 September 2007

Figures

Preface

This Field manual (FM) describes how logistics operations take place in the Brigade Support Area of Operations. It is primarily focused on how the brigade support battalion (BSB) performs its mission, but it also addresses the roles and functions of other sustainment elements within the brigade combat team (BCT) as well as those organizations external to the BCT that provide logistics and individual Soldier support services.

This field manual was written for BSB staff officers and non-commissioned officers..Knowing that many are assigned to battalion staffs prior to advanced formal education, this manual provides all a general idea of functions performed by each unit and staff section assigned to the BSB.

- Chapter 1 is a review of modular force logistics and the various types of brigade combat teams and support brigades.
- Chapter 2 explains the role of the BSB, including the headquarters company and staff, and briefly describes the role of the Aviation Support Battalion (ASB).
- Chapter 3 covers the organizational structure and function of the distribution company.
- Chapter 4 covers the role and organization of the field maintenance company.
- Chapter 5 provides detailed information on the brigade support medical company.
- Chapter 6 describes another key component of the brigade support battalion—the forward support company.

Logisticians and Soldier support specialists, enabled by technological advances, provide support essential to the BCT during the full spectrum of military operations: offense, defense, stability operations, and civil support. Sustainment facilitates uninterrupted BCT operations, and it is carried out through the replenishment of supplies, maintenance of equipment, and performance of other services. BCTs have a significant organic capability to sustain their own operations, which serves to ensure freedom of action, extend operational reach, and prolong endurance.

This publication applies to the Regular Army, the Army National Guard (ARNG)/Army National Guard of the United States (ARNGUS), United States Army Reserve (USAR), and Department of the Army (DA) civilian and contract personnel, unless otherwise stated. The proponent of this publication is US Army Training and Doctrine Command (TRADOC). Submit comments and recommended changes and the rationale for those changes that improve this publication on DA Form 2028 (Recommended Changes to Publications and Blank Forms) and forward it to Commander, USACASCOM, ATTN: G3-TDD , 2221 "A" Ave., Fort Lee, VA 23801-1809.

Chapter 1

Logistics Support to Modular Force Brigades

The brigade combat team (BCT) and support brigades are parts of the transforming Army which provides commanders with ready and relevant warfighting capabilities that are mission-tailored and scalable. Modular sustainment organizations, like brigade support battalions, provide a mix of capabilities that can be organized for any combination of offensive, defensive, stability operations, or civil support operations. This chapter provides an overview of modular logistic operations, the infantry and heavy BCTs, and the support considerations of the brigade support battalion (BSB).

SECTION I – MODULAR FORCE LOGSITICS

1-1. The BCT is the primary unit in the modular force. It is a fixed brigade-based, close combat unit that provides the division, land component, or joint task force commander with unique capabilities across the full spectrum of conflict. BCTs are optimized for combat operations but also are capable of conducting stability operations. They fight combined arms battles and engagements by employing every tactical means available. Their operations integrate the actions of maneuver battalions, field artillery, aviation, engineer, air and missile defense (AMD), combat air support, and naval gunfire to accomplish their missions.

1-2. The imperative of increased velocity reduces both organizational and materiel layering. Logisticians control the destination, speed, and volume of the distribution system. With in-transit visibility (ITV), total asset visibility (TAV), advanced materiel management, and advanced decision support system technology, logisticians have access and visibility over all items within the distribution system. This allows logisticians to divert, cross-level, and mass assets anywhere, anytime to support the maneuver commander. Logisticians maintain situational understanding of the battlefield via new technologies like the Battle Command Sustainment Support System (BCS3), which greatly facilitates logistics planning and execution.

1-3. To meet requirements, logisticians and human resources and medical support specialists draw on actionable data provided by command and control (C2) automation systems to determine the sustainability and supportability of current and planned operations. These systems provide near real time (NRT) logistics, human resources (HR), and medical information that link the BCT to the sustainment brigade and theater planners. Combined with an embedded, modular structure, staff officers and commanders have the capability to quickly and more accurately plan logistics operations.

Concept of Support

1-4. The BSB plans, coordinates, synchronizes, and executes replenishment operations in support of brigade operations. It distributes supply classes I, II, III, IV, V, VII, and IX; provides food service and Roles 1 and 2 Army Health System (AHS), as well as field maintenance and limited recovery. It maintains visibility of the theater distribution system, synchronizing the flow of throughput into the brigade's operational area.

1-5. Although BSB capabilities and structure differ somewhat depending upon the type of BCT (e.g. Heavy, Light, Stryker), core capabilities include maintenance, medical, supply, and distribution. BSBs provide responsive support to the brigade by positioning forward support companies (FSCs) with maneuver and fires battalions. The SBCT and support brigades are supported by organic BSBs.

1-6. BSBs provide a materiel carrying capability that enables the brigades to conduct sustained operations for a finite period of time. BSBs typically plan and execute replenishment operations in support of maneuver force battles and engagements. They are deliberate, time-sensitive operations conducted to replenish forward support companies with essential supplies, such as Class III (B) and Class V, to sustain the operations tempo. When required, a supporting sustainment brigade may augment BSB capabilities during BSB-planned and executed replenishment operations.

Distribution Operations

1-7. Designated distribution managers coordinate and synchronize logistics flow in accordance with (IAW) the commander's priorities and maximize throughput to units using all tools available to them. Distribution managers have asset and in-transit visibility (ITV) to optimize the distribution system within their areas of responsibility. Advanced information systems such as movement tracking system (MTS), battle command sustainment support system (BCS3) and advanced planning and optimization (APO) decision support tools provide this capability. ITV and communication packages allow distribution managers to direct or divert assets en route and shift assets quickly in order to meet changing distribution requirements.

Visibility

1-8. Visibility is a tenet of distribution. Distribution managers dedicate most of their work to gaining and maintaining visibility of networks, assets, processes, and capabilities throughout the distribution system. As summarized in FM 4-01.4, visibility ensures that the distribution system is responsive to customer needs. Experience has shown that Army leaders must be confident in the logistician's ability to support them. Timely and accurate visibility information provides logisticians with necessary information to distribute assets on time thus maintaining high confidence levels.

1-9. Visibility begins when the requirement is entered into the system and passed to the source of support. The information must be digitized and subsequently entered into the necessary logistics information systems. The key to digitizing information and ensuring it is accurately entered into the automated system is automating the process through bar coding and automated data entry. The next critical element to visibility is the capability to update the transport, storage, maintenance, or supply status of that particular item/shipment until it is received by the consumer. The information must be accessible to all users regardless of the service or the command requiring the data.

Situational Understanding

1-10. Situational understanding (SU) enables the logistician to meet the needs of the operational commander. SU is the complete understanding of the friendly situation, the enemy situation (as described by current intelligence), and the logistics situation through the use of information technology. Key elements of SU are:

- A common operating picture (COP) allows maneuver and logistics commanders to view the same data in near real time, enabling unity of command and unity of effort.
- An integrated, seamless information network bringing together ITV, unit requirements and COP in near real time and sharing the information across logistics functions, infrastructures and platforms.
- Timely and accurate asset visibility information allows the distribution of assets on time maintaining the critical confidence in the distribution system. Visibility begins where resources start their movement to the AO. ITV uses advanced automation, information, and communications capabilities to track cargo and personnel while en route.
- In addition to COP, liaison officers (LNOs) are often embedded at the maneuver brigade staff to pass current commander intent and mission changes to logistics elements.

Fusion of Logistics and Maneuver Situational Understanding

1-11. Effective logistics operations by the BSB are dependent on a high level of situational understanding (SU) and shared COP. SU enables the BSB commander and staff to maintain visibility of current and projected requirements, to synchronize movement and materiel management, and to maintain integrated visibility of transportation and supplies. BCS3, MTS, and Force XXI Battle Command Brigade and Below (FBCB2) are some of the fielded systems that the BSB uses to ensure effective SU and logistic support. These systems enable logistics commanders and staffs to exercise centralized C2, anticipate support requirements, and maximize battlefield distribution. It is critical that operations, plans and staff officers develop procedures and systems to collaborate and share information.

1-12. Logistics operations can be tailored in response to changes in tactical requirements. In most cases, the BSB will provide the supplies and services required by the supported unit at a specific point in time (scheduled delivery). For example, a typical day may include distribution to a battalion level distribution point for one customer cluster, to company/battery level for another customer cluster, and all the way to platoon/team level for a third cluster, while the fourth cluster receives no delivery, due to low or no requirements that particular day.

1-13. Supported unit commanders coordinate through their S3 and S4 staffs IAW current unit battle rhythm to fix the time and place for replenishment operations at a temporarily established point. Assets can be re-tasked if the situation demands. This approach, executed IAW centralized management, optimizes the employment of personnel.

Synchronization of Battle Rhythm and Logistics Operations

1-14. Support operations are fully integrated with the brigade battle rhythm through planning and oversight of on-going operations. Logistics and operational planning occurs simultaneously rather than sequentially. Incremental adjustments to either the maneuver or logistics plan during its execution must be visible to all BCT elements. The logistics synchronization matrix and logistics report (See Appendix A) are both used to initiate and maintain synchronization between operations and logistics functions.

SUPPORT METHODS

Unit (Battalion/Company/Platoon) Distribution

1-15. In unit distribution, supplies are configured in unit sets (battalion/company/platoon, depending on the level of distribution) and delivered to one or more central locations. Fuel trucks remain at the site to refuel unit vehicles as they cycle through the supply point. This technique makes maximum use of the capacity of BCT truck assets by minimizing delivery and turnaround time.

Supply Point Distribution

1-16. Supply point distribution requires unit representatives to move to a supply point to pick up their supplies. Supply point distribution is most commonly executed by means of a logistics release point (LRP). The LRP may be any place on the ground where unit vehicles return to pick up supplies and then take them forward to their unit. Occasionally, the LRP is the brigade support area (BSA) itself.

Refuel On The Move

1-17. The refuel on the move (ROM) method is conducted by having a fixed time and place to conduct the refuel operations IAW current unit battle rhythm. As a general rule, a ROM operation is established and conducted as part of a unit movement. A ROM may be built to support several types of units passing through a point sequentially.

Aerial Resupply (Deliberate, Fixed-Wing and Rotary Wing)

1-18. Aerial delivery is a viable option for cargo delivery in limited access or far forward areas or when delivery time is critical/sensitive. It may be a vital link in supporting reconnaissance, surveillance and target acquisition (RSTA) units or other small dispersed units throughout the operation.

Immediate Resupply

1-19. Immediate resupply, also referred to as emergency resupply, is the least preferred method of distribution of supplies. While some may be required when combat losses occur, requests for immediate resupply not related to combat loss indicates a breakdown in coordination and collaboration between the logistician and customer. If it is necessary, all possible means, including options not covered above, may be used. The battalion/squadron S4s, the BCT S4, and the BSB SPO must constantly and thoroughly collaborate to minimize this need. Emergency resupply that extends beyond BSB capabilities requires immediate intervention of the next higher command capable of executing the mission. In such case, the BCT S4 and BSB SPO immediately coordinate with the next higher echelon of support for the BCT.

Support to Separate Companies

1-20. The BCT may have an engineer company, a military intelligence company, an antitank company, and a network support company that do not operate under a battalion but are subordinate to the special troops battalion (STB). These companies, like the brigade HHC, are supported by the BSB regardless of where they are located on the battlefield. If one of these companies, or part of the company, is task organized to a maneuver battalion, it will retain from an FSC assigned to the BSB. The company commander must coordinate with the maneuver battalion's S4, the BSB SPO, the distribution and maintenance company commanders, and the supporting combat repair team (CRT) chief. Based upon the local situation and conditions, they may decide to integrate company's logistics requirements into the gaining battalion's logistic support structure.

Planning Considerations

1-21. The support concept for the BCT is based on a number of assumptions that must be considered as part of the military decision-making process (MDMP) process, and the availability of host nation and theater support contracts in areas such as transportation, life support, and facilities support as necessary. The food supply consists of MREs until food service capability arrives. Units attached or OPCON to the brigade must be accompanied by organic support elements. These elements will augment like elements in the BSB to provide required support. This must always be coordinated with the BSB SPO.

1-22. Sustainment stocks continue to flow during the initial, early entry buildup. However, resupply operations occur on an "as-needed" basis, rather than according to a fixed, cyclic schedule; delivery requirements may dictate less-than-full-truck loads which places an additional burden on transportation assets.

1-23. The Defense Logistics Agency (DLA) may provide bulk fuel, water, and food directly to units assigned to a brigade. This may be done either through pre-positioned stocks or DLA theater support contracts (e.g., into-plane contracts, into-bag contracts, into-truck contracts) after sources are inspected and approved by veterinary and preventive medicine (PVNTMED) personnel.

1-24. Refueling operations are planned and executed when BCT fuel status falls below a command specified level (example: 75 percent for RSTA elements; 50 percent all other units). When the situation warrants, Logistics Civilian Augmentation Program (LOGCAP) may be used to meet internal support requirements. LOGCAP is coordinated through the BSB SPO and the Army Field Support Brigade (AFSB).

Logistics Reporting

1-25. The logistics report is the internal status report that identifies logistics requirements, provides visibility on critical shortages, projects mission capability, and provides input to the common operating picture. In order to provide the support, unit commanders must coordinate closely with supporting and supported units using the logistics report. The report is forwarded from a unit to its higher headquarters and its supporting logistics headquarters. Commanders must dedicate the resources (personnel and time) to implement and leverage FBCB2 and BCS3 on log reports.

1-26. The logistics report will enable the higher command and support units to make timely decisions, prioritize, cross level and synchronize the distribution of supplies to sustain units at their authorized levels. The logistics report is the primary product used throughout the brigade and at higher levels of command to provide a logistics snapshot of current stock status, on-hand quantities, and future requirements. The logistics report gives the logistician the information and flexibility to manage requirements internally at the lowest level to ensure mission accomplishment.

1-27. The logistics report incorporates critical parts and supply status starting at company level. The intent is to identify the shortages at the lowest level first and then project the requirement to the next higher command and the support unit. The format for a modular force should incorporate organizational and direct support data on the same report to enable logisticians to fix issues at the lowest levels with the data being input and accessed locally. The Force XXI Battle Command Brigade and Below (FBCB2) forms the principal digital command and control system for the Army at brigade and below. The systems hardware and software are integrated into various platforms at brigade and below, as well as appropriate division and corps slices necessary to support brigade operations. All FBCB2 systems are interconnected through a communications infrastructure to exchange situational understanding data and conduct Command and Control. The logistics report is imported into BCS3 or the newly released Logisitics Report Tool (LRT) capability of BCS3. Either way it is BCS3 that supports and automates the Log Report.

1-28. The logistics report is not intended as a means of gathering the same information available in a logistics Standard Army Management Information System (STAMIS), nor to serve as the primary means of requisitioning commodities managed by a logistics STAMIS if BCS3 is available. The logistics report format is based upon METT-TC and should not overwhelm subordinate units with data submission requirements. A report that grows too cumbersome will overwhelm staffs and fail in high operational pace operations. It is important that this report is standardized and that units always provide input, regardless of their level of support.

1-29. Additional reports such as the maintenance readiness report (MRR), munitions report (MUREP) and petroleum report (REPOL) should not be added to reporting requirements to subordinate units below division-level when STAMIS and logistics report information satisfy information requirements.

1-30. At company level, the 1SG or designated representative is responsible for gathering the information from the platoon sergeants and submitting a consolidated report to the battalion S4. The 1SG can direct cross leveling between platoons and forecast requirements based on current balances and upcoming mission requirements. Some possible details to include in the logistics report are systems with an operational readiness rate below 60%, changes to anticipated expenditure rates, Class V status, and significant incidents. The primary means of gathering this information and submitting it to the battalion S4 is through the logistics report in FBCB2.

1-31. The battalion S4 is responsible for collecting reports from all companies and ensuring reports are complete, timely, and accurate. The battalion S4, with the support operations officer (SPO) and executive officer's (XO's) concurrence, makes the determination on which units receive which supplies. That decision is based on mission priority and the battalion commander's guidance. Upon receiving the logistics report, the company then validates external supplies to fulfill its requirements (where capable) and provides input to the logistics report on the adjusted balance of external supplies.

1-32. The adjusted balances of external supplies are added to the logistics report and returned to the battalion S4. The company also provides a coordination copy to the BSB's SPO. The battalion may include information such as STAMIS connectivity status, route and transportation node status, and distribution platform capabilities. The battalion S4 now has the complete logistics report and forwards this report to the brigade S4.

1-33. The brigade S4 is responsible for collecting reports from all battalions, including the BSB logistics report on internal supplies. The S4 ensures that reports are complete, timely, and accurate. Prior to the forwarding a consolidated report to the BSB SPO, the brigade S4, with brigade executive officer's concurrence, determines which units receive which supplies. Their decision is based upon mission priority and the brigade commander's guidance. Upon receiving the logistics report, the SPO conducts a Brigade Logistics Synchronization meeting. The BSB SPO then disseminates the external supplies to fulfill battalion requirements (where capable), synchronizes distribution, and provides input to the logistics report.

1-34. The SPO input to the logistics report focuses on the adjusted balance of external supplies owned by the BSB and forecasting resupply requirements into the brigade. Some other possible information to include would be stockage levels, inventory on hand and in bound, and supply performance statistics. The adjusted balances of external supplies and forecasted requirements are added to the logistics report and returned to the brigade S4. The BSB SPO also provides a courtesy copy to the supporting sustainment brigade SPO. The brigade S4 now has the complete logistics report and forwards this report to the division G4. Once validated, the logistics report is used to update the synchronization matrix. The end result should be a refined logistics report containing an accurate forecast of logistics requirements for use by operational level support organizations. The updated logistics report and logistics synchronization matrix complement paragraph 4 and annex I of the operations order (OPORD), or fragmentary order (FRAGO).

1-35. The division/corps G4 is responsible for collecting reports from all task organized brigades and ensuring reports are complete, timely, and accurate. The division/corps may add information such as changes to theater opening and changes to anticipated expenditure rates.

Echelons above Brigade Support and the Request Process

1-36. All logistics requirements (less medical) beyond the BSB's ability are either furnished by or coordinated through the supporting sustainment brigade. The sustainment brigade SPO is the POC for BCT logistics requirements above the capacity of the BCT BSB. Like the other BCTs, the sustainment brigade supports the BCT on an area basis. When properly task organized, the sustainment brigade is capable of supporting BCT requirements for all classes of supplies (less Class VIII), maintenance, field services, contracting and other logistics requirements. Through its distribution capability, the sustainment brigade normally provides distribution of supplies to the BCT BSB in support packages. The sustainment brigade operates Ammunition Supply Points (ASPs) for the distribution of Class V to the BCTs.

1-37. The BSB is designed to be reinforced by echelons above brigade (EAB) sustainment organizations. The goal is to reduce the amount of supplies and equipment in the AO. Through the Sustainment Brigade, the BSB exploits regionally available resources through joint, multinational, HN, or contract sources for certain bulk supplies and services. A key logistics reach organization responsible for coordinating contracted support and for providing other national strategic logistics capabilities is the AFSB. The AFSBs are part of Army Sustainment Command (ASC), a major subordinate command of the US Army Materiel Command (AMC).

1-38. If resources must be contracted, the SPO ICW with the BDE S-4, prepares an acquisition ready packet which details the specific requirement(s), then passes the requirements to the supporting contracting officer (KO) who works within the context of the Army/joint contracting framework for the operation.

SECTION II – BRIGADE ORGANIZATION AND FUNCTIONS

1-39. Brigade combat teams operate as part of a division. The division acts as a tactical headquarters controlling up to six BCTs in combat operations plus a number of supporting functional brigades. The division assigns the BCT its mission, AO, and supporting elements, and coordinates its actions with other BCTs of the formation. The BCT may be required to detach subordinate elements to other BCTs of the division. In its principal role as a combined arms maneuver unit, the BCT closes with and destroys the enemy by combining reconnaissance, surveillance, target acquisition, long range fires, maneuver, and the support of joint and other Army units. It uses every available military and interagency means to gain information superiority, and to ensure understanding of every aspect of the terrain, weather, enemy, civil concerns, and friendly forces prior to and during execution.

INFANTRY BRIGADE COMBAT TEAM (IBCT)

1-40. The IBCT conducts offensive, defensive, and stability operations. The IBCT's core mission is to close with the enemy by means of fire and maneuver to destroy or capture enemy forces, or to repel their attacks by fire, close combat, and counterattack. The IBCT provides specialized capabilities as an independent maneuver force or as a subordinate maneuver component to division or corps in major combat operations (MCO). In a smaller-scale contingency (SSC), the IBCT provides a corps or joint task force a combat team that deploys rapidly, executes early in forced entry operations, and conducts offensive operations immediately upon arrival to prevent, contain, stabilize or resolve a conflict, or to promote peace.

1-41. During a peacetime military engagement (PME), the IBCT conducts programs or training exercises with other nations to assist in shaping the international environment and improve interoperability with treaty partners or potential coalition partners. The IBCT consists of the Brigade Special Troops Battalion, two infantry battalions, Reconnaissance, Surveillance, Target Acquisition and Fires Battalion, and Brigade Support Battalion. Figure 1-1 shows the units that make up the IBCT.

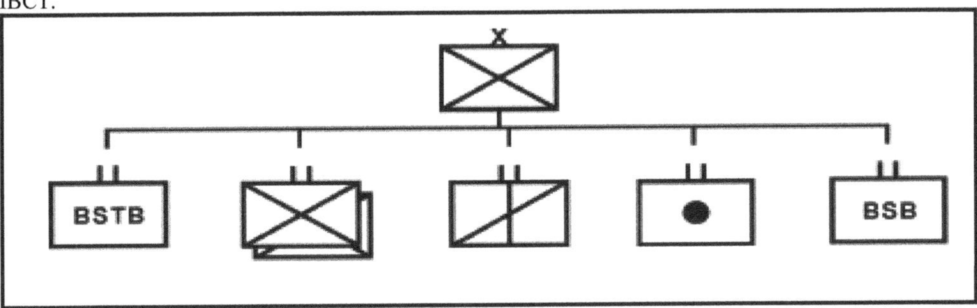

Figure 1-1. Infantry Brigade Combat Team

1-42. The BSB of the IBCT is structured very similarly to the BSB of the HBCT. The two distinctions are that instead of an armored reconnaissance squadron and two combined arms battalions it supports a reconnaissance/surveillance/target acquisition battalion, two infantry battalions and a fires battalion. It also contains mobility elements, one element in the BSB and one in the infantry battalion FSC, that are collectively intended to move one battalion of infantry in one lift.

STRYKER BRIGADE COMBAT TEAM (SBCT)

1-43. The BSB of the SBCT contains a headquarters and headquarters company, a distribution company, a field maintenance company and a medical company. It does not contain FSCs.

HEAVY BRIGADE COMBAT TEAM (HBCT)

1-44. HBCTs are designed to conduct offensive, defensive, and SO. Their core mission is to close with the enemy by means of fire and maneuver to destroy or capture enemy forces, or to repel their attacks by fire, close combat, and counterattack. They are designed to conduct offensive, defensive, and SO. The HBCT is a full-spectrum combat force that can be used in all operational environments and against all threats. The HBCT provides significant capabilities as a subordinate maneuver component to division or corps commanders in MCO. The HBCT includes a Brigade Special Troops Battalion, Combined Arms Battalion, Reconnaissance Squadron, Fires Battalion, and Brigade Support Battalion. Figure 1-2 shows how the HBCT is organized.

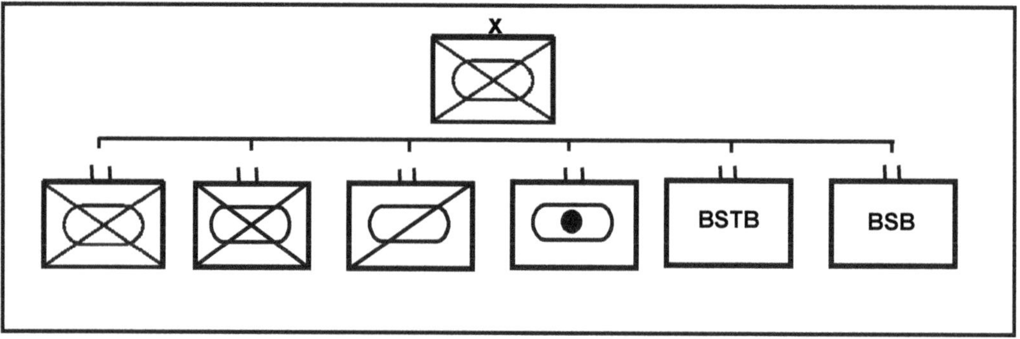

Figure 1-2. Heavy Brigade Combat Team

1-45. The BSB of the HBCT contains a headquarters and headquarters company, one distribution company, one field maintenance company, one forward support company (FSC) to support an armored reconnaissance squadron, two identical FSCs to support the two combined arms battalions, and one FSC to support a fires battalion.

SUPPORT BRIGADES

1-46. A mix of multifunctional support brigade supports theater army, corps, and division commanders. These supporting brigades include the battlefield surveillance brigade (BFSB), combat aviation brigade (CAB), maneuver enhancement brigade (MEB), fires brigade, and sustainment brigade. These brigades are task organized to support BCTs and carry out specific tasks in support of echelons above BCT. (See Figure 1-3) A division involved in major combat operations should be supported by all five types of support brigades.

1-47. Most support brigades are not fixed organizations. All support brigades except the CAB are designed around a base of organic elements, to which a mix of additional capabilities is added based on the factors of METT-TC. The brigade headquarters includes the necessary expertise to control many different capabilities. Each type of support brigade's base includes organic signal and sustainment capabilities.

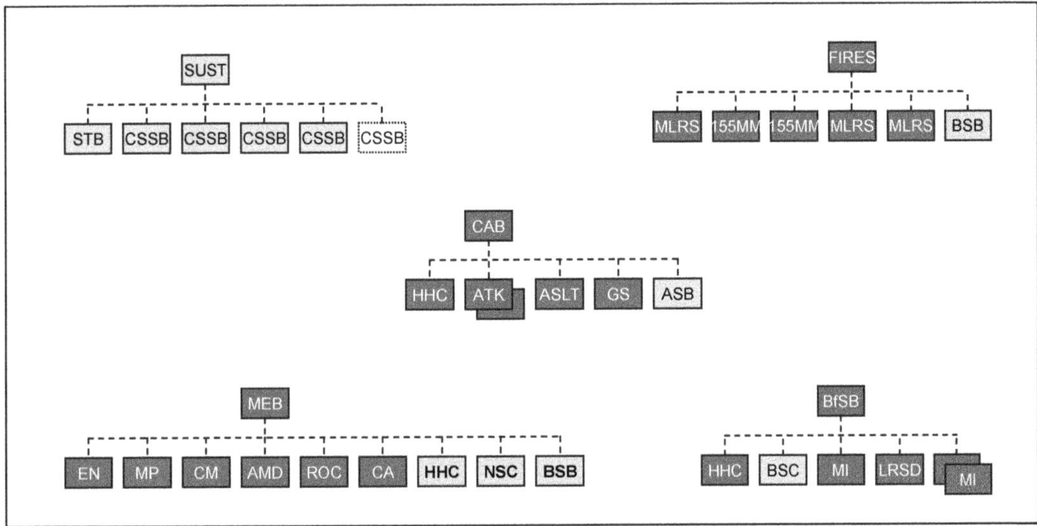

Figure 1-3. Support Brigades

Battlefield Surveillance Brigade (BFSB)

1-48. The mission of the BFSB is to conduct reconnaissance and surveillance (R&S) to answer the division commander's information requirements (IR), enabling him to focus joint elements of combat power. The brigade also provides assets to enhance the R&S capabilities of other units in the division, including BCTs. (FM 3-55.1) The information it collects focuses on the enemy, terrain and weather, and civil consideration aspects of METT-TC which feed the development and update of the COP. The BFSB is normally assigned, attached or OPCON to a division. It is organized with a Military Intelligence Battalion, a Reconnaissance and Surveillance (R&S) Battalion.

1-49. The BFSB contains a Brigade Support Company (BSC), not a BSB. The BSC contains capabilities that are generally commensurate with a BSB, but is sized as a company based on the BFSBs support requirements. It contains a headquarters platoon, a distribution platoon with field feeding, class III and water sections, and a robust maintenance platoon. The BSC provides limited logistics and field maintenance support to the BFSB. The BFSB S4 is responsible for planning and coordinating the additional logical support and field maintenance.

1-50. The BFSB Brigade Support Company (BSC) is dependent upon elements of the Sustainment Brigade for replenishment operations, Battle Damage Assessment Repair (BDAR), combat spares, additional field maintenance support (to include CE and COMSEC equipment), bulk fuel, and water production.

Combat Aviation Brigade (CAB)

1-51. CABs synchronize operations of multiple aviation battalions task organized to provide reconnaissance, security, close combat attack, interdiction attack, air assault, and air movement operations in support of ground forces under the headquarters to which it is assigned (FM 3-04.111). This can be a JFLC, a corps, or a division. Based on priorities and missions, the CAB can also collaborate directly with a supported BCT or other brigade for operational details of the support required.

1-52. The CAB is tailorable to the mission, containing both manned and unmanned systems, and can support multiple BCTs. CABs can be configured as heavy, medium, or light in accordance with the numbers and types of assigned aircraft.

1-53. The CAB Aviation Support Battalion (ASB) provides distribution of CL I, II, III(B), IV, V, and IX, ATHP, water purification and storage and limited transportation. It also provides Aviation Intermediate Maintenance (AVIM).

Maneuver Enhancement Brigade (MEB)

1-54. The MEB provides task organized forces in support of Army division, echelon above division (EAD), joint, interagency, or multinational headquarters. The MEB operates across the full spectrum of operations to support, reinforce or complement offensive and defensive major combat operations and can support or conduct stability or civil support operations. The MEB is designed as a C2 headquarters with a multifunctional brigade staff that is optimized to conduct maneuver support operations. Maneuver support operations integrate the complementary and reinforcing capabilities of key protection, movement and maneuver, and sustainment functions, tasks, and systems to enhance freedom of action. The MEB contains no organic units other than its headquarters and headquarters company (HHC), network support company (NSC), and brigade support battalion (BSB). Each MEB is uniquely tailored with augmentation for its directed mission. (See FM 3-90.31.)

1-55. An MEB typically includes a mix of several types of battalions and separate companies which may include civil affairs (CA); chemical, biological, radiological, and nuclear (CBRN); engineer; explosive ordnance disposal (EOD); and MP units. It may also contain military intelligence (MI) assets, tactical combat force (TCF), and air and missile defense (AMD) units. The MEB is not a maneuver brigade although it can be assigned an AO and control terrain. The MEB receives, commands, and controls forces to conduct operations. These brigades will typically be called upon to control terrain and potentially facilities as well. MEBs provide capabilities to enhance freedom of movement and maneuver for operational and tactical commanders.

1-56. The MEB BSB provides support to the MEB by providing and/or coordinating CL I, II, III, III(P), IV, V, VII, and IX supplies, field maintenance, and limited transportation support. It also coordinates for additional transportation needs identified by the brigade. The MEB BSB is dependent upon the Quartermaster Collection Company (MA) for Mortuary Affairs Support. The BSB of the MEB contains a headquarters and headquarters company, a distribution company and a field maintenance company. It does not contain FSCs or a medical company.

Fires Brigade

1-57. The fires brigade plans, prepares, executes, and assesses operations to provide close support, shaping, and decisive fires for the division. The fires brigade is the primary executor of Army and Joint fires in areas not assigned to BCTs. It is capable of employing Army and Joint air surface and aerially delivered fires as well as incorporating Special Operations Forces (SOF), Information Operations (IO), Civil Affairs (CA), and Army Airspace Command and Control (A2C2) elements. The fires brigade gives the division/corps commander a headquarters to plan, synchronize, and execute strike, counterstrike, and reinforcing fires across the division.

1-58. The fires brigade also has the necessary command and control structure to integrate attached ground and air maneuver forces and function as a maneuver headquarters for limited operations. Fires brigades differ from Army of Excellence (AOE) field artillery organizations in their ability to reconnoiter, detect, and attack targets and confirm the effectiveness of their fires. They also are characterized by networked intelligence, robust communications, and systems that facilitate the efficient application of fires. The fires brigade is capable of being a supported or supporting unit and providing and coordinating Joint lethal and non-lethal fires including Information Operations (IO). Fires brigades also have the necessary fires support and targeting structure to effectively execute the entire decide, detect, deliver, and assess (D3A) process.

1-59. The fires brigade is routinely assigned to a division and normally designated as the division Force Field Artillery Headquarters (FFA HQ). Since the fires brigade is the only Army field artillery unit above BCT, it will likely execute missions for any Joint, Service or functional HQ, Marine Force (MARFOR), Joint Forces Air Component Commander (JFACC) as well as multinational HQ.

1-60. BSB provides support to the Fires Brigade by providing and/or coordinating CL I, II, III, IV, V, VII, and IX supplies, Roles 1 and 2 AHS) support, limited field maintenance and limited transportation support. The BSB operates an Ammunition Transfer holding Point (ATHP) in the brigade support area (BSA), and a Quartermaster Collection Company (MA) for Mortuary Affairs Support. The BSBs of the Fires Brigade contains a headquarters and headquarters company, a distribution company, a field maintenance company, and FSCs designed to support the particular type of field artillery battalion of which the brigade is comprised (i.e., Paladin, MLRS, towed). It does not contain a medical company.

Sustainment Brigade (SUST BDE)

1-61. Sustainment brigades are subordinate commands of the TSC, designed to provide C2 of theater opening, distribution, and sustainment operations within an assigned area of operation. All sustainment brigade HQ are identical in organizational structure and capabilities. The building blocks of the SUST BDE are three to seven combat sustainment support battalions (CSSBs) and /or functional logistics battalions conducting replenishment operations that allow combat forces to replenish routinely. For more information on the SUST BDE refer to FMI 4-93.2.

SECTION III – SUPPORT OPERATIONS IN FULL SPECTRUM OPERATIONS

Offense

1-62. The BCT conducts, or participates in, movements to contact (MTC), attacks, exploitations, and pursuits. The BCT may participate in a division pursuit or exploitation by conducting an MTC or attack. The BCT's reconnaissance squadron and ISR assets do not negate the need to conduct the traditional MTC. However, the actual techniques used during MTC may be modified to fit the capabilities found within each of the BCTs.

1-63. During the offense, the BSB supports the BCT with more robust and more rapid replenishment than previous support battalions prior to the modular force. With the BSB assigned to the brigades that it supports, the brigade commander has the ability to place these assets at his discretion. Logisticians should plan for increased use of Class III products during offensive operations.

1-64. If offensive momentum is not maintained, the enemy may recover from the shock of the first assault, gain the initiative, and mount a successful counterattack. The logistic priority must maintain the momentum of the attack. These considerations apply to some degree to all offensive operations. The change from one type of operation to another, such as from a hasty attack to a pursuit, does not require a major shift in logistics plans and procedures. However, the priorities and requirements for support may change. The task force XO, assisted primarily by the S-4, organizes the task force's logistic assets to permit uninterrupted support. The main purpose of the offense is to maintain the momentum of the attack.

Defense

1-65. BCT defensive operations break the momentum of the enemy's attack while maintaining the capability to shift to the offense with little notice. The BCT will conduct an area or static defense, dynamic mobile defense, or retrograde in a variety of threats and terrains. The tactical mobility of the BCT makes it well suited for the dynamic defense. The support battalion commander supports the wide range of options available to the brigade commander conducting defensive operations. Without sacrificing support, the support battalion commander locates BSB support points out of reach of possible penetrations in protected and concealed locations. Elements are also out of the way of potential retrogrades. BSB units disperse as much as possible without impairing command and control or security. They use built-up areas as much as possible. The support battalion commander in conjunction with the brigade S-3 plans ADA coverage and emphasizes passive measures.

1-66. The BSB is poised to quickly react to needs on defense with the capability of setting up an ammunition transfer and holding point (ATHP) within its distribution company that can hold three days of supply for the BCT or support brigade. It is capable of quickly adapting to the changing needs of supported units in defensive postures. Logisticians should plan for greatly increased ammunition expenditure during defensive operations.

Stability Operations

1-67. Army logistics enables the commander to execute his mission and sustain the force. This is true throughout the range of Army operations, logistics forces may be employed in nonstandard tasks or in quantities disproportionate to their normal roles. Like all other elements, they must be capable of self defense, particularly if they deploy alone or in advance of other Army forces. The principles of Army Sustainment are discussed in FM 4-0.

1-68. Sustainment of stability operations often involves supporting U.S. and multinational forces in a wide range of missions. It can be conducted in support of a host nation or interim government or as part of an occupation when no governments exist. Stability operations may range from long-term humanitarian and civic assistance (HCA) missions to major short notice peace enforcement. Some stability operations may involve combat. Tailoring supplies, personnel and equipment to the specific needs of the operation is essential. Stability operations include:

- Establish civil security.
- Establish civil control.
- Restore essential services.
- Support to governance.
- Support to economic and infrastructure development.

1-69. Host-nation support, contracting, and local purchases are force multipliers in many of these operations. Logisticians should plan for increased use of Class III products during offensive operations. Situations that lack optimal sustaining capabilities may require using nonstandard logistics. They may augment or replace existing logistic capability. They can reduce dependence on the logistic system, improve response time and free airlift and sealift for other priority needs. Contracting personnel should precede the main body of Army forces if feasible. Nonstandard logistics may be employed for—

- Limited supplies such as Classes I, II, III, IV, VII, and IX.
- Services such as catering, maintenance and repair, sanitation, and laundry.
- Rental services such as mobile communications.
- Transportation.

1-70. The Logistics Civilian Augmentation Program (LOGCAP) provides the ability to rapidly contract logistics support requirements in a theater of operations. See AR 700-137 for LOGCAP information. Commanders can expect that contractors will be involved in stability operations. The management and control of contractors differs from the command and control of soldiers and Department of the Army (DA) civilians. During military operations, soldiers and DA civilians are under the direct command and control of the military chain of command. Commanders can direct soldier and DA civilian task assignment, special recognition, and disciplinary action. However, they do not have the same control over contractors. The terms and conditions of the contract establish relationships between the military and the contractor. Commanders and staff planners must assess the need for providing operational area security to a contractor and designate forces to provide security when appropriate. The mission of, threat to, and location of the contractor determines the degree of protection needed.

Civil Support Operations

1-71. Civil support is Department of Defense support to U.S. civil authorities for domestic emergencies, and for designated law enforcement and other activities (JP 1-02). Civil support is Department of Defense support to U.S. civil authorities for domestic emergencies, and for designated law enforcement and other activities (JP 1-02). Civil support includes operations that address the consequences of natural or man-made disasters, accidents, terrorist attacks, and incidents in the United States and its territories. Army forces conduct civil support operations when the size and scope of events exceed the capabilities or capacities of domestic civilian agencies. Usually the Army National Guard is the first military force to respond on behalf of state authorities. In this capacity, it functions under authority of Title 32, U.S. Code, or while serving on state active duty. The National Guard is suited to conduct these missions; however, the scope and level of destruction may require states to request assistance from Federal authorities.

SUMMARY

1-72. The Modular Force has allowed Army units to become more responsive and flexible as Army commanders required. The Commanders' needs can be met with greater efficiency, and decreased response times. There will no longer be a need to disassemble large unitized structures to create specialized task forces that leave behind valuable manpower. The BCT and Modular Force brigades are parts of the transforming Army which provides commanders with ready and relevant warfighting capabilities that are mission-tailored and scalable. BSBs provide a mix of capabilities that can be organized for any combination of support operations.

This page intentionally left blank.

Chapter 2

The Role of the BSB

The BSB, in all of its variations, is a full spectrum-capable organization organic to maneuver brigades and some support brigades operating at the tactical level. As such, its operations are an inherent part of the overall brigade operational planning and execution cycle. The BSB command group synchronizes and integrates requirements of the brigade with the sustainment brigade in conjunction with the division G4. This chapter describes the basic organization of the BSB. It also describes the headquarters and headquarters company command and staff organizations along with their basic functions.

BSB Mission

2-1. The mission of the BSB is to plan, prepare, rapidly deploy, and execute the uninterrupted flow of tactical-level logistics and AHS support to the particular type of brigade it supports. The BSB is trained and equipped to support the brigade's requirements for full spectrum operations which include offense, defense, stability operations, and civil support. The BSB and its subordinate units must be fully prepared to conduct any combination of these primary operations.

2-2. Each BSB is tailored to support a specific type of brigade. While most types are designed with essentially the same structures and capabilities, the exact capabilities in each vary based on the type of supported brigade. For example, the combat aviation brigade contains an aviation support battalion that is different from other types of BSBs. For the organizational structure of BCT's refer to FM 3-0.

2-3. The BSB of the HBCT contains a headquarters and headquarters company, one distribution company, one field maintenance company, one forward support company (FSC) to support an armored reconnaissance squadron, two identical FSCs to support the two combined arms battalions, one FSC to support a fires battalion, and a brigade support medical company (BSMC).

2-4. The BSB of the IBCT is structured very similarly to the BSB of the HBCT. The two distinctions are that instead of an armored reconnaissance squadron and two combined arms battalions it supports a reconnaissance/surveillance/target acquisition battalion and two infantry battalions. It also contains mobility elements, one element in the BSB and one in the infantry battalion FSC, that are collectively intended to move one battalion of infantry in one lift.

2-5. The BSB of the SBCT contains a headquarters and headquarters company, a distribution company, a field maintenance company and a medical company. It does not contain FSCs.

2-6. The BSB of the MEB contains a headquarters and headquarters company, a distribution company and a field maintenance company. It does not contain FSCs or a medical company.

2-7. The BSBs of the Fires Brigade contains a headquarters and headquarters company, a distribution company, a field maintenance company, and FSCs designed to support the particular type of field artillery battalion of which the brigade is comprised (i.e., Paladin, MLRS, towed). It does not contain a medical company.

2-8. The Battlefield Surveillance Brigade (BFSB) contains a Brigade Support Company (BSC), not a BSB. The BSC contains capabilities that are generally commensurate with a BSB, but is sized as a company based on the BFSB support requirements. It contains a headquarters platoon, a distribution platoon with field feeding, class III and water sections, and a robust maintenance platoon. The BSC provides limited logistics and field maintenance support to the BFSB. The BFSB S4 is responsible for planning and coordinating the additional logical support and field maintenance.

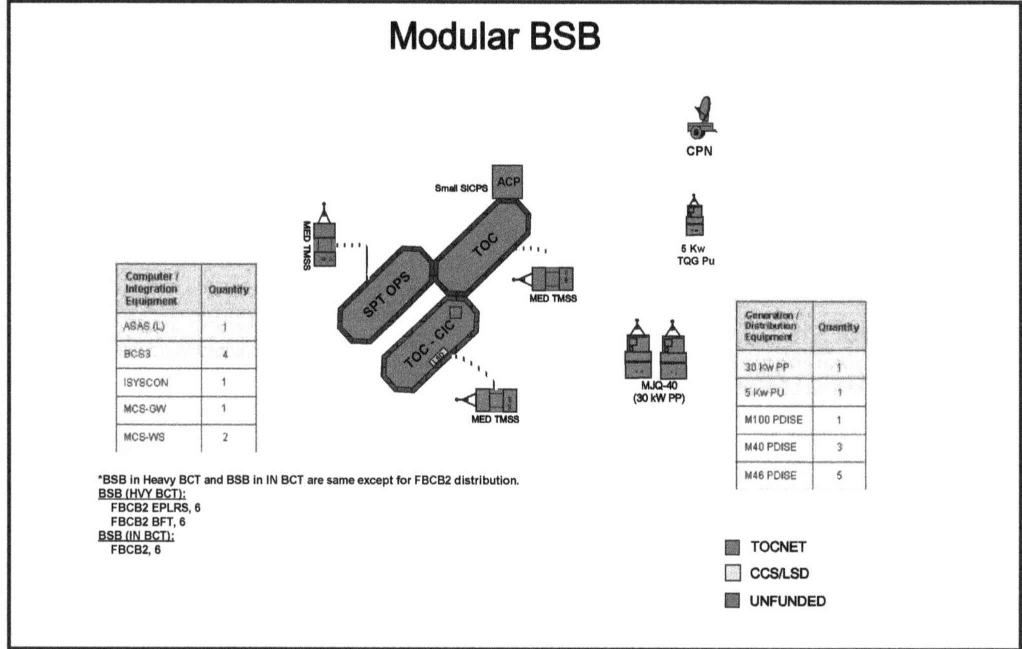

Computer / Integration Equipment	Quantity
ASAS (L)	1
BCS3	4
ISYSCON	1
MCS-GW	1
MCS-WS	2

Generation / Distribution Equipment	Quantity
30 Kw PP	1
5 Kw PU	1
M100 PDISE	1
M40 PDISE	3
M46 PDISE	5

Figure 2-1. Brigade Support Battalion TOC

CAPABILITIES OF THE BSB

2-9. Although the extent and scope of capabilities differ somewhat depending on the type of BSB, each BSB generally has the following capabilities which align with the warfighting functions. The BSB command group provides command and control to include administrative actions for units assigned and attached to the BSB. A typical BSB TOC layout is displayed in Figure 2-1.

2-10. The distribution company provides transportation support to the brigade, moving move fuel, water, dry cargo and ammunition. The distribution supply capability includes general supplies (less Class VIII), repair parts, bulk petroleum, ammunition, water purification (distribution company), and water distribution (FSC). The distribution company provides supply support to the BSB, the brigade headquarters, and the brigade special troops battalion. The FSCs provide this capability for their respective supported battalion.

2-11. The field maintenance company provides field maintenance support to the BSB, the brigade headquarters, and the brigade special troops battalion. The FSCs provide this support to their respective supported battalion.

2-12. BSBs that contain a medical company provide Role 2 medical care to include behavioral health support to all units within the brigade. Organic medical support within the brigades that do not have a medical company is limited to battalion and aid stations Role 1 medical treatment facilities and medical evacuation capability embedded in each of the maneuver battalion HHCs.

2-13. FSCs are assigned to ICBT, HBCT, and Fires Brigade and provide distribution, supply, limited transportation, maintenance, and field feeding to the supported battalion.

2-14. Other capabilities include:

- Religious Support is provided by the unit ministry team within the BSB HHC to units assigned to the BSB.
- Protection of the BSA is the responsibility of the BSB which plans, conducts, coordinates and maintains the BSA security.
- Human resources support for the BSB is embedded within the BSB S-1. Financial management support is provided on an area support basis by FM units attached to the sustainment brigade.
- The BSB has the capability to support the movement and maneuver of the brigade such as deployment to an intermediate staging base in preparation for offensive operations.

SECTION I – BSB HEADQUARTERS AND HEADQUARTERS COMPANY

2-15. The BSB Headquarters and Headquarters Company contains the BSB battalion headquarters, command group and staff organizations. The battalion headquarters provides command and control for all organic and attached units of the brigade support battalion. Its capabilities include providing all human resources support for units organic or assigned to the BSB. The staff conducts planning, provides direction, and oversees logistics operations for all assigned and attached units in the brigade combat team. It commands and controls all units in the BSA for security and terrain management.

HEADQUARTERS COMPANY ROLE

2-16. The headquarters company provides C2 and oversight of all company level operations for the BSB HQ. The company HQ is responsible for the Soldiers assigned to the BSB HQ. In addition to those defined by regulation, the HQ commander is responsible for developing the HQ occupation plan, ensures local HQ security, and plans, coordinates, and executes HQ movements.

SECTION II – STAFF ORGANIZATIONS AND FUNCTIONS

COMMAND GROUP

2-17. The command group of the BSB provides command and control oversight for all units assigned and attached to the BSB that are responsible for support to the BCT. The command group consists of the BSB battalion commander, battalion executive officer, command sergeant major (CSM) and commander's driver.

BSB COMMANDER

2-18. The BSB commander is the senior logistics commander and single logistics operator for the BCT. The BSB commander directs all units organic or attached to the BSB and also has command and control of all elements in the BSA for security and terrain management. The commander provides subordinate elements with clear missions, tasking, and statement of his intent. The commander is also responsible for unit training, morale, welfare, and recreation (MWR) activities, coordinating food service, billeting, field sanitation, supply, and field maintenance for organic equipment and coordinating AHS support.

2-19. The commander, with the HHC staff, supervises the activities of subordinate units. They ensure that decisions, directives, and instructions are implemented and that the BCT commander's intent is being fulfilled. The BSB commander and staff advise the BCT commander on logistic support as required. The battalion commander also provides logistics assets required to support the BCT, clear and understandable commander's intent and mission guidance, a personal estimate of the situation and decisions while reviewing running estimates, performing COA analysis, and deciding upon the COA that best supports the BCT mission.

BSB Executive Officer

2-20. The BSB executive officer is the commander's chief of staff. The XO directs, coordinates, supervises, trains, and synchronizes the work of the staff and ensures effective and prompt staff actions. The commander normally delegates authority to the executive officer for executive management of coordinating and special staff officers. The XO must understand the commander's intent and ensure the BSB staff implements it. The XO monitors the status of all subordinate units and ensure that status is provided to the BSB commander.

2-21. The duties of the executive officer include management of the commander's critical information requirements (CCIR), organization of the staff into functional and integrating cells and working groups when required. Other XO duties include supervising the creation of and approval of the Logistics Report, the BSB command post, its operations, and positioning within the BSA.

2-22. The executive officer also determines liaison requirements with the BCT headquarters and supervision of the liaison officers ensuring quality of work from the staff officers and staff fusion throughout the planning, preparation, and execution phases. Another responsibility of the XO is synchronization of the BSB staff during the military decision making process, establishing and maintaining the staff planning guidelines.

Command Sergeant Major

2-23. The BSB command sergeant major (CSM) is a member of the commander's personal staff and is the senior noncommissioned officer (NCO) of the command. The CSM is responsible for providing the commander with personal, professional, and technical advice on enlisted Soldier matters and the NCO corps as a whole, and is usually located at the BSB main command post (CP).

Headquarters Staff

2-24. Although there are minor variations in BSB staff structures, the key staff sections are the S1 section, consolidated S2/3 section, S4 section, S6 section, support operations section , unit ministry team (UMT) and the Sustainment Automation Support Management Office (SASMO).

2-25. The BSB headquarters directs the C2, communications systems, and ISR functions of the BSB. Generally, the BSB headquarters provides the following: Planning, direction, and supervision of logistics for all units assigned or attached to the BCT.

2-26. The BSB headquarters also provides unit-level personnel and religious services for units of the battalion, planning and direction of rear operations and limited area security as assigned by the supported brigade commander, information and advice to the supported brigade commander and staff on support capabilities provided by the battalion, field feeding and ration storage.

2-27. The BSB headquarters is also responsible for maintaining situational understanding using C2 information management systems. These systems provide location and configuration, total asset visibility, ITV, and overall connectivity to supported and adjacent units, and higher headquarters.

2-28. The BSB main CP centrally controls distribution operations for the BCT. The main CP also coordinates for the protection of the BSA under direction of the BSB S2/3.

S1 Section

2-29. The S1 serves as the BSB principal staff officer for human resources support and other issues impacting on the health, morale, and welfare of BSB personnel. This includes manning, HR services, personnel support, and HR staff operations and planning. The S1 coordinates medical, religious, and legal support and is responsible for developing the HR support portion of OPLAN/OPORD.

2-30. HR support is embedded within the BSB. HR support includes, personnel accountability, strength reporting, casualty operations, personnel information management, personnel readiness, essential personnel services, casualty operations, postal operations, MWR, and command interest programs. The S1 relies on the brigade S1 for direct coordination with HRC on replacement and assignment of BSB personnel. The brigade S1 also supports the BSB S1 by providing or coordinating HR support beyond the capabilities of the BSB S1 or brigade S-1. See FM 1-0, Human Resources Support, for additional information on HR support tasks and functions.

S2 SECTION

2-31. The S2 is the coordinating staff officer for matters concerning the enemy, environment, counterintelligence and other threats that could affect logistic operations. The S2 also serves as the security officer for the battalion. Because the BSB staff has a consolidated S2/3 section, the S2 officer functions as a staff element under the S3. The S2 has lead responsibility for intelligence preparation of the battlefield (IPB), and is responsible for intelligence readiness, intelligence tasks, intelligence synchronization and other intelligence support.

2-32. The S2 is responsible for obtaining classified maps and is responsible for the preparation of the intelligence annex to OPLANS/OPORDS, daily intelligence summary for subordinate units, intelligence estimates and updates, paragraphs 1a and 1c and the intelligence annex of the BSB OPLAN/OPORD. This staff section works in nominating, tracking and updating priority intelligence requirements (PIR), conducting continuous IPB, identifying intelligence collection requirements, coordinating tactical intelligence activities between subordinate units and the BCT S2.

2-33. The S2 also maintains a weather factor analysis matrix, performing and distributing analysis of the AO. The S2 prepares situation, event, and decision support templates, reports on captured enemy materiel, writes intelligence updates for all convoys in order to provide current enemy situation, likely areas of enemy activity, and new enemy TTPs. The S2 reports pattern analysis of all main supply routes (MSRs) and alternate supply routes (ASRs) in the BCT AO, assists the S3 in tracking route status, and provides input to the Battalion Logistics Report.

S3 SECTION

2-34. The S3 officer is the operations, security, and training officer. The S3 is responsible for internal BSB operations. The S3 advises and assists the BSB commander in tactical planning, coordinating and supervising the communications, operations, training and security functions of the battalion. The S3 must work closely with the BSB support operations officer to assist in the development of the concept of support for the brigade. The S3 is responsible for writing and reviewing the battalions tactical SOP.

2-35. The S3 section monitors the tactical operations of the BSB, makes recommendations to the commander, publishes orders, and supervises implementation of plans and orders. It obtains maps and prepares overlays. It positions units within the BSA and plans BSA security that includes planning equipment and personnel for the base cluster reaction force to include the traffic circulation plan for the BSA. The section ensures the BSA security plan is integrated into the overall BCT security plan. The section also plans and coordinates tactical movements, receives closing reports, and supervises appropriate staff activities during movement.

2-36. The S3 officer supervises the operations of the plans-operations branch. The S3's duties include developing the unit task organization in coordination with BSB SPO, planning and executing operations security and CBRN defense and training, and developing the force module packages for deployment of the BSB.

2-37. The S3 issues warning orders to all assigned or attached elements, does the coordinating with BCT S2 and S3 staffs on the tactical situation in the BCT area, prepares contingency plans, analyzes operational data and reports for conformance to directives and commander's intent, and coordinates for combat, general, and geospatial engineering support.

2-38. The duties of the S2/3 operations sergeant include operating the brigade support area FM radio net, advising on operational area security, coordinating with the supporting EOD company for removal or rendering safe of unexploded ordnance. He coordinates with the engineers for engineer support to route or area clearance; other mobility support, survivability operations to improve protection within the BSB, and necessary geospatial support.

2-39. Internally the S2/3 operations sergeant supervises security training and provides input to the Battalion Logistics Report as required.

2-40. The CBRN NCO prepares the CBRN defense annex to OPLANs/OPORDs and SOP. The NCO also supervises the CBRN program, prepares the tactical CBRN plans, and assists the S3 in planning of CBRN related logistics efforts. He conducts CBRN vulnerability analysis and assessments, maintains the radiation exposure status for subordinate units, plans for decontamination support to subordinate units and collects data for and preparing CBRN reports.

S4 Section

2-41. The S4 plans the coordination and execution of internal logistic support requirements for the battalion. The BSB S4 provides technical supervision for unit level support within the battalion. Specifically, the S4 coordinates transportation for administrative moves and internal supply functions, determines supply requirements (except medical), determines supply priorities for publication in OPLANs and OPORDs, and coordinates the requisition, acquisition, and storage of supplies and equipment. The S4 also monitors and coordinates the collection and distribution of surplus and salvage supplies and equipment, assists the S3 in the execution of deployment plans for the headquarters and subordinate units, maintains status of internal logistics situation, assists units in the development of their unit movement plan, and screens transportation requests and passes to Distribution Operation Section.

2-42. Internally within the battalion the S4 will monitor field feeding, property book activities, maintenance operations, unit basic loads (UBLs), equipment operational status and the status of requisitions for equipment and supplies. The BSB S4 also acquires and assigns facilities, and develops the Logistics Report for the battalion.

S6 Section

2-43. The S6 is responsible for determining requirements and exercising staff supervision over communications services related to BSB operations. The S6 advises the commander, staff, and subordinate units on communications and Automation Information System (AIS) matters. The primary function is ensuring the integrity of the FM and digital C2 communications network. Signal specialists install, operate, and maintain communications equipment and ensure communication links with higher, adjacent, subordinate, and supported units. They plan and implement backup means of communications and ensure radio communications exist during a move between the start point (SP) and release point (RP), and along the route of march. They also develop and implement a BSA security communications system to connect elements such as the dismount point, observation posts (OPs), LRPs, and the quick reaction force (QRF).

2-44. The S6 is responsible for the full range of tasks associated with network management, systems administration, and systems/software security for all tactical automation. The S6 also uses the CSS Automation Information Systems Integrated (CAISI) to establish a secure wireless local area network (LAN) for the logistics sensitive but unclassified (SBU) network. The S-6 contributes to the LOGSTAT as required.

2-45. As systems administrator and system/software security manager, the S6 performs all tasks normally associated with IT operations ranging from issuing passwords and installing anti-virus software to performing network management functions. The S6 supervises communications security (COMSEC) and controlled cryptographic items (CCI) activities. The S6 resolves applications problems with logistics STAMIS and BCS3. The S6 is also responsible for installing and operating LANs in support of BSB operations. The S6 will monitor and submit AIS status to the Logistics report as required.

Unit Ministry Team

2-46. The BSB UMT consists of one chaplain and one chaplain assistant. The mission of the BSB UMT is to provide and perform unit religious support to Soldiers and authorized civilians as directed by the BSB commander. The UMT provides area and denominational religious support IAW the brigade religious support plan under the technical supervision of the BCT chaplain. They have two roles: religious leader and staff officer. As a religious leader the chaplain executes the religious support mission, to ensure the free exercise of religion for Soldiers and authorized personnel. The chaplain is a personal staff officer and serves as an advisor to the BSB commander on matters of religion, moral atmosphere of the command, morale as affected by religion, and the impact of indigenous religions on operations.

2-47. The chaplain assistant is a Soldier trained to assist the chaplain in providing religious support. Under the direction of the chaplain, the chaplain assistant coordinates and synchronizes all tactical, logistic, and administrative actions necessary to carry out religious support operations. The chaplain assistant coordinates and manages protection for the BSB UMT.

Sustainment Automation Support Management Office (SASMO)

2-48. The SASMO installs and monitors the Combat Service Support Automated Information System Interface (CAISI) and Very Small Aperture Terminals (VSAT) network and satellite operations to provide assured, unclassified but sensitive, non-secured communications. SASMO provides user support in sustaining and operating the systems used in the sustainment brigade and supported battalions (especially those functional battalions that do not have an organic SASMO.

2-49. SASMO support includes all installation, testing, loading, and troubleshooting of systems software, limited hardware, user owned communications devices, and monitoring user training programs and new equipment fielding. The office also establishes the unclassified wireless network and domain-name service and monitors network traffic and protection status. It provides software maintenance support to organic BSB elements. The SASMO will monitor and input STAMIS status to the Logistics Report as required.

SECTION III – SUPPORT OPERATIONS

2-50. The BSB support operations officer (SPO) is the principal staff officer for coordinating support for all units assigned to the brigade. The support operations officer provides planning, preparation, and C2 of the execution of all BSB sustainment operations in the brigade's AO. The support operations officer also provides technical supervision of all sustainment operations conducted by the BSB and is therefore the key interface between supported units and the sustainment brigade. He is responsible for communicating BSB sustainment requirements to the sustainment brigade as these requirements become known. Requirements are determined in coordination with the brigade S1, brigade S4, and BSB S2/3. The support operations officer performs logistics preparation of the battlefield and advises the commander on the relationship of support requirements to support assets available. The support operations officer plans and monitors support operations and makes necessary adjustments to ensure support requirements are met, and provides the status of SPO tracked systems and materiel as required to update the BSB Logistics Report.

2-51. The relation between the BSB SPO and the BSB S3 cannot be overemphasized. These two officers and their respective sections must have full cooperation in order to properly plan the sustainment support to the brigade. The method by which this is accomplished is not as important as the actual cooperation, and the two sections must use the method that is the most effective for them. Current and future operations must be taken into account and responsibility for each area fixed and acted on as a team.

SUPPORT OPERATIONS

2-52. The support operations section, under the direction of the support operations officer, provides centralized, integrated, and automated command, control, planning, preparation, and execution of all support operations within the brigade. Although the section's structure varies slightly by type of BSB, and the types and number of personnel assigned will vary, generally the section consists of plans, operations, transportation, food service/field feeding, maintenance management, ammunition, mortuary affairs, AHS support (except fires, BFSB and MEB), and materiel management officers and NCOs.

2-53. The support section is responsible for coordinating logistics provided to the BCT and provides the technical supervision for the external logistics mission of the BSB. It is the key interface between the supported units, the BSB and the sustainment brigade. Its primary concern is customer support and increasing the responsiveness of support provided by subordinate units. This section coordinates and directs external support requirements, provides technical expertise to supported units, and synchronizes support requirements to ensure they remain consistent with current and future operations. The section coordinates with the S1/4 to track available logistics assets and coordinates with the S2/3 for operational locations and schedules of the supported units.

2-54. The support operations section acts as the distribution management element for the BSB, functioning as a distribution management center (DMC) for the brigade. It synchronizes operations within the distribution system to maximize throughput and ensure priorities are executed in accordance with the BCT commander's guidance. The distribution managers maintain situational understanding of the distribution system and act as the fusion center for distribution-related information. Distribution management resources also include a limited management capability to monitor MTS, FBCB2, TC-AIMS II, BCS3, legacy STAMIS/ Global Combat Support System – Army (GCSS-A), and daily battle loss reports to anticipate requirements. Requirements that exceed BSB capabilities are coordinated with higher supporting headquarters and utilize reach operations. The support operations section takes information from the distribution system to create a synchronized picture of the flow of units, personnel, and materiel into and throughout the AO.

2-55. The support operations section must leverage the automated information systems available to it. BCS3 is the commander's sustainment command and control system and has the capability to provide vast amounts of information to the staff if properly implemented. It provides current status of all units within the brigade in near-real time, provides projected combat power of units to allow the section to anticipate needs, and in-transit visibility of supplies. Commanders must allocate the time and resources to train with, understand, and prepare the system for use.

PLANS

2-56. The plans officer, with support from other plans personnel on the section, prepares detailed input to OPLANs and FRAGOs for the SPO. The plans officer works closely with the BCT S4 and supported battalion S4s to coordinate future support requirements and locations with supported units. As required the plans personnel collocate with the BCT S4 to execute concurrent planning operations. He also develops the logistic estimate and support plans for future operations. The plans officer recommends/incorporates all technologies/automation, combat unit requirements, unit historical data, current/future logistics posture, mobility data, and commander's guidance into the development of the support plan.

OPERATIONS

2-57. The operations officer develops the support operations order and associated logistics annexes to all plans and orders. He has directive authority over subordinate BSB units during the performance of current operations and brigade support operations. He, along with other section operations personnel, maintains the running estimate. Through the use of interoperable automation and communications, they perform daily management functions and fuse logistics requirements for the support/distribution operations section.

Transportation Operations

2-58. The transportation officer plans and manages movement and distribution operations. The section collects, collates and analyzes support information for the plans branch and individual commodity sections and develops the movements annex for plans and orders. It plans for and controls the use of ground transportation assets specifically allocated or attached for logistics and distribution missions. In addition to accomplishing their specific commodity/management missions, all other managers will channel information to the transportation officer to improve the total distribution system visibility, and to allow for overall coordination, prioritization and decision-making by the support operations officer.

Food Service/Field Feeding

2-59. The BDE Food Service Warrant Officer and SR Food Operations NCO oversee and ensure all field feeding operations within the BSB. They ensure that adequate rations are available and or of the appropriate type based upon the operational situation of the brigade. The food service warrant works closely with and advises the field feeding teams within the BDE (FSCs, BSB, and BSTB).

Maintenance Management

2-60. The maintenance management personnel provide maintenance oversight of the field maintenance company and FSCs maintenance sections. They ensure integrated, automated maintenance management for combat vehicles, automotive ground support equipment, communications electronics equipment and missile equipment. The maintenance management personnel also plan and forecast maintenance and related material requirements based on future operational plans and coordinates the disposal of enemy equipment.

Ammunition Operations

2-61. The ammunition NCO provides oversight of all brigade ammunition replenishment operations. They must work closely with the ATHP section of the distribution company and with the FSCs to ensure prompt and adequate support to the brigade. The ammunition NCO must be keenly aware of the brigade's ammunition requirements and have awareness of controlled supply rates that affect the brigade operations. The ammunition personnel must coordinate with the sustainment brigade for ammunition resupply. As directed by the battalion commander the ammunition warrant officer may be moved to the S3 plans section to assist in battalion operations planning.

Medical Operations

2-62. The medical operations officer, in concert with the brigade surgeon's section and medical company commander, plans for all AHS support operations within the brigade. The medical operations officer must take into consideration placement of all AHS support assets within the brigade. They must also coordinate the ordering, receipt, and distribution of CL VIII and blood products within the BCT. This section also coordinates with the brigade and as appropriate, division surgeon sections for all AHS support issues affecting the brigade.

Mortuary Affairs Operations (MA)

2-63. The mortuary affairs NCO coordinates with the sustainment brigade or other MA units in the area to understand the MA concept of operations, to include location of all mortuary affairs collection points. The mortuary affairs NCO provides guidance to all brigade units on the initial search and recovery, tentative identification, evacuation, and decontamination of remains and personal effects (PE).

MATERIEL MANAGEMENT

2-64. The materiel management NCO and Specialist provide supervision and management of general supplies (less Class V) within the brigade. They monitor the on-hand stocks within BSB companies, determine requirements, coordinate local purchase, retrograde, and distribution of supplies. They also provide oversight of parts requirements and projections of parts availability.

SECTION IV – COMMAND AND CONTROL

ROLE OF THE COMMANDER

2-65. The commander's role is to establish a command climate for his unit, prepare it for operations, direct it during operations, and continually assess subordinates. The sustainment commander visualizes the nature and design of operations through estimates and input from subordinates. He describes support operations in terms of time, space, resources, purpose, and action, employing intent, commander's critical information requirements, and mission orders for planning, preparation, and mission execution.

2-66. The BSB commander and staff use MDMP to prepare for and supervise the execution of orders. The MDMP process is outlined in FM 5-0. An abbreviated version of the process appears here. The process is a continuous one; the support battalion commander and staff are always involved in estimating and planning. However, the focus becomes more precise when the support battalion receives a mission.

2-67. The BSB commander analyzes the mission, usually receiving planning guidance and a restated mission from the brigade commander. When he receives or deduces the mission, the support battalion commander and staff begin mission analysis. The BSB staff identifies the tasks required to accomplish the mission. It issues a warning order to all support battalion elements, along with the support battalion planning guidance.

2-68. The BSB staff uses planning guidance to prepare estimates. Therefore, the support battalion commander ensures that the nature of his planning guidance does not bias running estimates. The support battalion commander and staff plan continuously. Yet, it is not until they receive the BCT commander decision on the tactical employment of brigade units that they finalize the concept of operations. Working with the brigade staff, the support battalion staff develops the logistics and AHS concept of support.

2-69. The BSB staff determines what type, quantity and priority of logistics and AHS support is required and available, and where these resources are located and when they are available to supported units. Such logistics and AHS support planning is as detailed as time permits. Sound SOP and contingency plans greatly assist in the development of specific plans. When SOPs are comprehensive, they have to change only to accommodate specific requirements or circumstances. In any case, planning concentrates on those areas most vital to successful mission accomplishment of the supported brigade.

2-70. On the basis of staff estimates, the support battalion commander determines the supportability of courses of action to accomplish the mission. Once the support battalion staff finalizes the support plans, the XO gives guidance on preparation of the OPORD/OPLAN. The S-2/S-3 consolidates the input. He then publishes and distributes the OPORD/OPLAN after the support battalion commander approves it.

2-71. After the S-2/S-3 distributes the OPORD/OPLAN, the support battalion commander and staff supervise its execution. The primary purpose of the staff is to assist subordinate units to carry out the intent of the support battalion commanders' order. The support battalion staff refines plans and orders as the situation changes. Information comes back to the command section through reports and personal observations of the battalion/company commanders and staff and the FSC commanders. On the basis of this information, it evaluates instructions as required.

Command And Control (C2) Information System

2-72. Commanders cannot exercise C2 alone except in the simplest and smallest of units. Even at the lowest levels, commanders need support to exercise C2 effectively. At every echelon of command, each commander has a command and control system to provide that support. A command and control system is the arrangement of personnel, information management, procedures, and equipment and facilities essential for the commander to conduct operations. Digitized information systems now being fielded will increase the complexity of C2. Commanders must commit personnel and time resources to fully implement automated C2 systems such as BCS3, FBCB2, and MTS. For additional information on C2 refer to FM 6-0.

Organizational Relationships Process

2-73. To perform their C2 functions, the BSB commander and staff develop and maintain relationships with supporting, supported and subordinate organizations, as well as with the BCT and Division G4. The brigade commander and his staff plan all aspects of brigade operations. The brigade S-4 assists in the area of logistics. The brigade S4 provides logistics (less CL VIII) information to the commander and acts as the brigade logistic planner (less CL VIII). As such, he coordinates the status of supplies and equipment with the maneuver battalion XO and S-4s. He also coordinates with representatives of support elements attached and assigned to the brigade.

BSB And Supported Brigade Units

2-74. The BSB commander and staff also form a close relationship with the supported battalions and other attached and assigned units. This close relationship with supported units ensures planners integrate support battalion operations with the operations of the supported forces. The BSB and supported units work out the day-to-day details of logistics operations in the brigade. These include specific requirements and time schedules. For routine operations, the BSB companies also develop relationships with supported units such as FSCs, the BSTB support platoons, and medics.

2-75. In addition to its relationship to the brigade, the BSB has terrain management and security responsibilities. Unless otherwise stated by OPORD, it has operational control over units located within the BSA and responsibility for the security of the BSA. Exact responsibilities will be determined by OPORD or FRAGO from the brigade S-3 who has overall staff responsibility for the security of the brigade.

BSB Headquarters And Subordinate Companies

2-76. The BSB commander maintains close personal contact with his subordinate company commanders. He depends on them to provide timely information on the status of their companies. In addition, the company commanders understand the BSB commander's intent to perform their roles with initiative. They enhance this understanding through frequent face-to-face discussion.

2-77. The BSB has from three to seven subordinate companies depending on the type of BSB. All BSBs have a headquarters and headquarters company, a distribution company which is the link through the SPO to the sustainment brigade, a field maintenance company which provides base field maintenance support to the BSB and to the supported brigade.

2-78. The HBCT, IBCT, and SBCT BSBs have a medical company which provides Role 2 medical, mental health, and force health protection to the BSB and the supported brigade. The HBCT BSB and the IBCT BSB each have four forward support companies that provide multifunctional logistics support to a maneuver battalion; one per armored reconnaissance battalion, one for each of two combined arms battalions and one for the fires battalion. The fires brigade BSB has up to four forward support companies each of which is designed to support a specific type of artillery unit; self-propelled, towed, HIMARS, or MLRS.

2-79. The distribution, field maintenance, and medical company commanders are likely to operate in the vicinity of the support battalion CP to facilitate coordination. However, they do not tie themselves to one spot. They command their companies from the locations where they can best assess and influence the support operation. These commanders use verbal orders, radio, visual signals, or wire among themselves, the support battalion staff, their platoon leaders, and the supported elements.

BSB and Echelon Above Brigade (EAB) Units

2-80. A number of EAB units may operate in the brigade area such as an engineer battalion, military intelligence teams, military police companies, air and ground ambulance units, Special Forces Operational Detachment-Alpha (ODA), and medical units. If the EAB units are in the brigade AO and the number of personnel and items of equipment to be supported are small enough, the BSB supports them on an area basis. If the numbers are substantial or dispersed, the sustainment brigade may need to support these elements, or provide augmentation to the BSB. In all cases, these EAB units receive AHS support from the nearest medical facility regardless of unit affiliation. If the BCT deploys with a division, EAB units operating in the BCT AO normally obtain support from the sustainment brigade or logistics task force employed in the division's AO.

2-81. The support battalion normally ties directly into the theater logistics system. The BSB SPO coordinates with the support operations staff of the sustainment brigade and/or the CSSB designated for support. Coordination may include ammunition support, sustainment maintenance to the FMC, designated field services (CEB, laundry teams), bulk fuel support, general supply support and mortuary affairs support.

2-82. The support battalion transportation officer goes through the brigade S-4 to request transportation support from the supporting movement control team (MCT). An MCT is normally collocated with division headquarters and will request transportation support from supporting sustainment brigade through another MCT or the MCB.

The Aviation Support Battalion (ASB)

2-83. The ASB is the primary aviation logistics organization in the Combat Aviation Brigade (CAB). The ASB has been optimized to support the CABs field support company/troops, aviation maintenance companies/troops (AMC/AMT) and the brigade's HHC. In addition, it has been resourced to support simultaneously from two locations. The ASB heavy variant is designed to support AH-64 aircraft in addition to UH-60, CH-47, and medical evacuation (MEDEVAC) lift assets. The ASB medium organization must support both AH-64 and OH-58D aircraft in addition to MEDEVAC and lift assets while the light organization supports OH-58D and lift airframes. At the theater level, the ASB is organized without the network support company (NSC).

2-84. Figure 2-2 depicts the organizational composition of the ASB. It consists of four companies; the headquarters and support company (HSC), the distribution company, the aviation support company (ASC), and the NSC. See chapters 5, 6, 7, and 8 for a further description of the ASB companies.

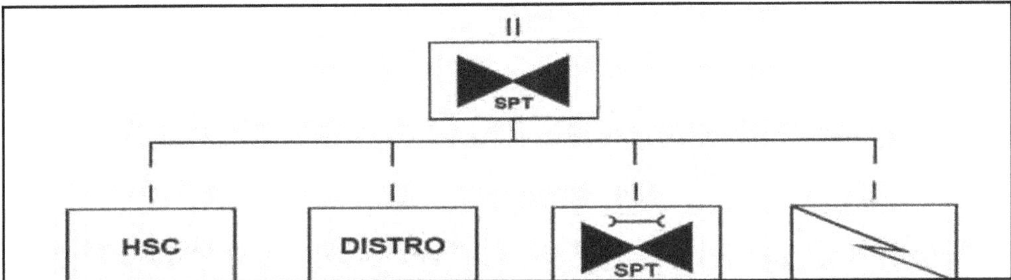

Figure 2-2. The Aviation Support Battalion

2-85. The ASB distributes supply classes I, II, III, IV, V, and IX. It performs field maintenance and assists in recovery operations, both air and ground, and has the medical assets to conduct AHS support at a Role 1 medical treatment facility for the CAB. It carries the replenishment stocks for the CAB (generally one day of supply (DOS) for most classes of supply except for Class III(B) and Class V where it is one combat load for the CAB's maneuver battalions and squadrons). The ASB SPO plans and coordinates for the CAB's logistics requirements in conjunction with the brigade S4 during the CAB's military decision making process (MDMP). The ASB executes replenishment operations for the FSC/FSTs and the AMC/AMTs in concert with the CAB's operational plan. The ASB is also the parent battalion headquarters for the NSC that supports the CAB headquarters.

SUMMARY

2-86. The BSB, in all of its variations, is a complex and capable organization. It has the challenging task of supporting a brigade in full spectrum operations. The BSB may function in a dispersed manner, with some BSB elements close to maneuver units and others in or near the BSA, possibly in a non-linear, non-contiguous battlefield, and may be assigned other missions by the BCT Cdr deemed necessary to the success of the brigade. The BSB commander, staff, and subordinate companies must have a complete understanding of both the brigade mission and the support the BSB provides in order to ensure success on the battlefield.

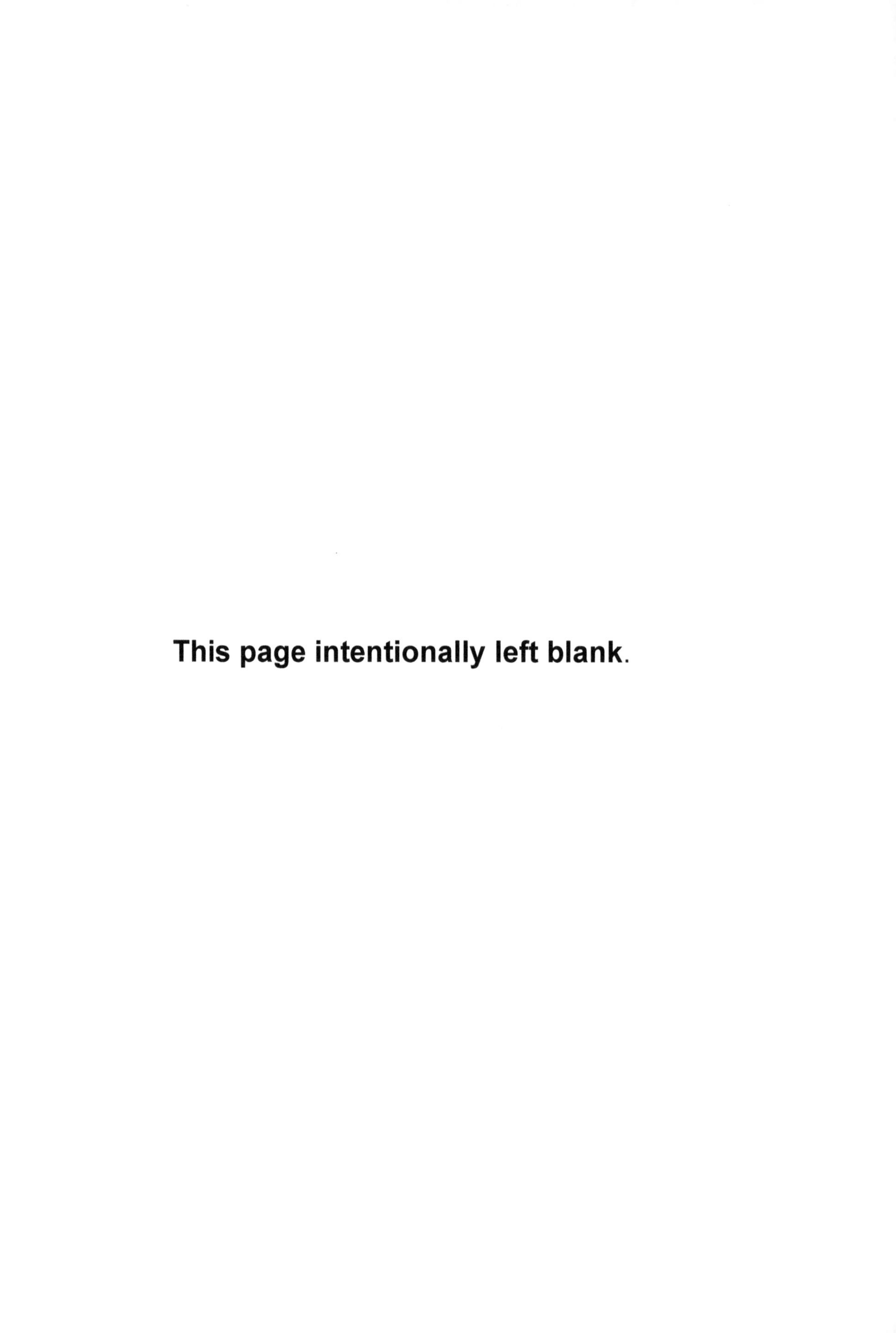

This page intentionally left blank.

Chapter 3

The Distribution Company

The brigade support battalion's distribution company is the primary supply and transportation hub of the BCT. It manages the distribution of supplies to the brigade. It provides receipt, storage, and issue of Class I, II, III, IV, IX and unclassified maps. It also conducts Class V operations with its ammunition transfer and holding point (ATHP) section and provides transportation for elements of the brigade and the brigade ASL. In contrast, the distribution company has no maintenance section and features a combined fuel and water platoon.

SECTION I – MISSION

3-1. The mission of the distribution company is to provide transportation, supply, Class III, and water support to the BCT. This unit is employed in the brigade support area (BSA) and operates as part of the BSB with subordinate elements that operate throughout the BCT area.

3-2. This unit provides the planning, direction, and supervision of supply distribution and transportation support to the BCT, daily receipt, temporary storage, and issue of Supply Classes I, II, III, IV, V and IX to the BCT. This unit also provides for the transportation of cargo and the water purification and distribution for the brigade.

3-3. Distribution companies are also a vital link in the retrograde of materiel. Retrograde of materiel is the return of new, reparable or salvageable materiel from the owning/using unit back through the distribution system to the source of supply, directed ship-to location and/or point of disposal. Retrograde of materiel is as important as the forward distribution of materiel. Retrograde functions include turn-in/classification, preparation, packing, transporting and shipping. To ensure these functions are properly executed, commanders enforce supply accountability and discipline, and maintain proper packing materials.

SECTION II – ORGANIZATION

3-4. BSB distribution companies have three platoons consisting of a distribution platoon, supply platoon and a fuel and water platoon, as shown in Figure 3-1. Distribution companies in the different types of BSBs are similar, with the major difference being a more robust fuel section in the HBCT BSB, a more robust ATHP Section in the MEB BSB, and a Mobility Section added in the IBCT BSB for movement of personnel. The distribution company has the capability to conduct replenishment operations in support of the BCTs tactical mission, which does not require the supported battalions' FSCs to go to the BSA for replenishment. The distribution company receives supplies coming from the supporting sustainment brigade with the capability to store these supplies and issue them to units within the BSA, to the FSCs, and the forward maintenance teams (FMTs).

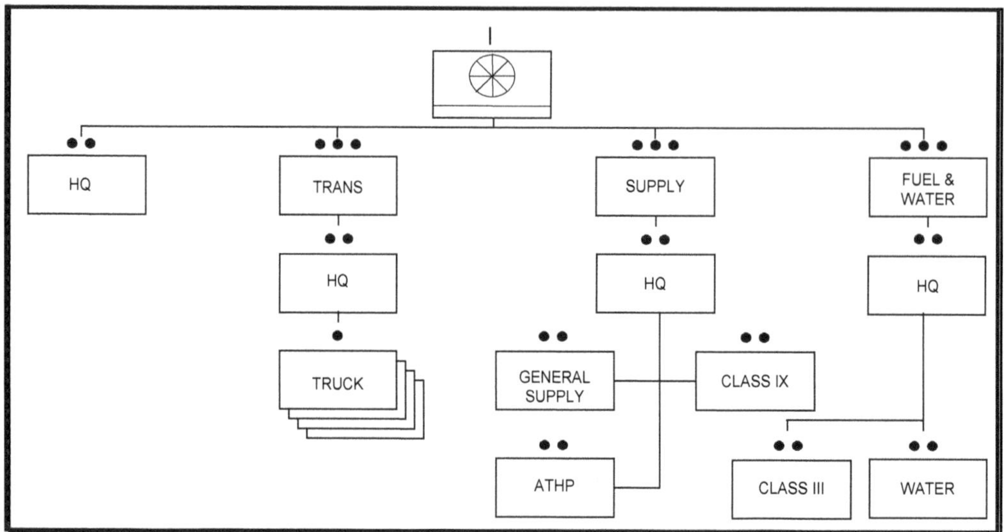

Figure 3-1. Distribution Company

Company Headquarters

3-5. The company headquarters provides C2 for all of the company's operations. The headquarters provides information and advice concerning distribution operations to the BSB commander and support operations staff. It also is responsible for operating the company's net control station (NCS).

Company Commander

3-6. The company commander's responsibilities are to execute the BCT and BSB commanders' distribution plans in support of the BCT commander's scheme of maneuver. The commander must manage task organization and employment of all distribution assets, collaborate and coordinate with the BSB SPO and BCT S4 to determine the best distribution concept of support for the BCT, and maintain continual communications with higher, lower, and adjacent units.

Executive Officer

3-7. The company XO is the company second in command and the primary internal logistics planner and coordinator. The XO and the company headquarters section serve as the company staff and operate the company CP. The company XOs conducts continuous battle tracking and ensures that timely tactical reports are sent to the BSB TOC. Other responsibilities include:

- **Assumes command of the company in absence of commander.**
- In conjunction with the 1SG, plans and supervises the company logistics and defense effort before, during, and after the battle.
- Prepares the company OPORD for the commander.
- Conducts tactical and logistics coordination with higher, adjacent, and supported units.

3-8. As required, the XO will also assist the commander in issuing orders to the company, headquarters, attachments, and conduct additional missions as required. These may include serving as OIC for the quartering party, company movement officer, or company training officer.

First Sergeant

3-9. The 1SG is the company senior NCO and normally is its most experienced Soldier. The 1SG is the commander's primary logistics and tactical advisor and is an expert in collective skills. The 1SG helps the commander and XO to plan, coordinate, and supervise all logistics activities that support the company mission. The 1SG operates where the commander directs or where his duties require him. The 1SG's specific duties include:

- Executing and supervising routine operations.
- Collecting rollup data for the company LOGSITREPs and PERSITREPs and forwarding to the battalion administrative and logistics operations center (ALOC).
- Conducting training and ensuring proficiency in individual and collective tasks.
- Receiving incoming personnel and assigning them to subordinate elements as needed.
- Establishing and maintaining foundations for company discipline.
- As necessary the First Sergeant will serve as quartering party NCOIC.
- Movement of soldiers killed in action to the supporting mortuary affairs collection point.

Truckmaster

3-10. The truckmaster is the operations assistant to the operations officer and the company commander. The truckmaster assists in the coordinating, supervising, and controlling of company transportation. The truckmaster participates in convoy planning and enforces march discipline. He supervises, through the unit dispatcher, all dispatching and routing of company vehicles. He assists the operations officer in preparing reports, maintains visibility of employed company assets and personnel, and supervises vehicle operations and driver training. The truckmaster coordinates with platoon sergeants and the maintenance sergeant to ensure complete knowledge of status and vehicle availability and maintains a file of unit accident reports.

Supply Sergeant

3-11. The supply sergeant requests, receives, issues, stores, maintains, and turns in supplies and equipment for the company. He reports all supply actions and requirements to the commander and coordinates them with the 1SG and the battalion S4. His specific responsibilities include inventory and financial management procedures, including ordering, receiving, issuing and storing of unit supplies. He monitors company operations and the tactical situation to anticipate logistics requirements and provides this information to the company 1SG in preparation for the LOGSITREP report. The supply sergeant also controls the company cargo truck, resupplies the water trailer, and supervises the supply clerk and the unit armorer.

CBRN Specialist

3-12. The CBRN specialist assists and advises the company commander in planning for and conducting operations in a CBRN environment. The CBRN specialist plans, conducts, coordinates, and/or supervises CBRN defense training with the 1SG and covers such areas as decontamination procedures and use and maintenance of CBRN-related equipment.

Armorer

3-13. The armorer performs field maintenance on company small arms and is responsible for evacuating weapons to the BSB field maintenance company when required. In addition, the armorer normally assists the supply sergeant in his duties. As an option, the armorer may serve as the driver of the 1SG's vehicle to make him more accessible for weapons repair and maintenance.

SECTION III – OPERATIONS

TRANSPORTATION PLATOON

3-14. The transportation platoon provides direct transportation support to the brigade and distribution of supplies to the FSCs. There are a differing number of truck squads in the BSBs, the HBCT and SBCT BSBs each have four, the IBCT BSBs have three, the MEB BSBs have two and the Fires BDE BSBs have one. The IBCT BSBs also have mobility squads to move personnel around the area of operations. There are no dispatchers assigned to the Fires BDE and SBCT BSBs.

3-15. The transportation platoon headquarters provides command and control, supervision and technical guidance to tactical truck and/or mobility squads performing motor transport support, supply delivery, and distribution operations. The platoon also provides transportation support for the distribution of supplies to each FSC.

3-16. Although the transportation platoon leader works for the distribution company commander, he receives battalion support operations taskings through the battalion S-3. Transportation platoon truck squads provide 24-hour motor transport, supply delivery, and distribution operations to brigade units. The mobility sections provide 24-hour personnel movement for the rifle companies in the infantry battalions.

3-17. The BCTs transportation units can expect to move frequently in response to changes in requirements. FM 55-30 has more detailed information on transportation units and operations.

SUPPLY PLATOON

3-18. The supply platoon provides Class I, II, III (P), IV, V, VII, and IX support to the brigade. The supply platoon receives, stores (limited) and issues Class II, III (P), IV, and IX. It also receives and distributes, in conjunction with (ICW) with the Transportation Platoon, Class I from the field ration issue point, and receives and issues Class VII as required. The platoon also maintains limited Class II, III (P), IV and IX ASL for the brigade. The ATHP section supports the brigade with Class V and operates the brigade ammunition transfer/holding point (ATHP). It stores the third combat load for supported units and provides these supplies to the supported battalions FSCs. The BSB is 100% mobile to keep pace with the companies it supports; therefore the supply platoon maintains a mobile storage capability.

3-19. The supply platoon headquarters provides command, control and supervision to the stock control, Class IX, general supplies, subsistence and ATHP sections. The supply system technician is assigned to this section to supervise assigned and attached personnel and is responsible for the receipt, storage, issue, security and inventory of the items that flow through the warehouse.

Materiel Control and Accounting Section

3-20. This section provides ASL stock control, receipt, storage, and issue management. The materiel control supervisor must ensure that daily start-up and closeout procedures are followed IAW the schedule of operations established by the supporting headquarters. Automated document processing and warehousing operations will be conducted IAW AR 710-2 and unit SOP.

3-21. The materiel control and accounting section should be collocated to facilitate on-site item management and inventory control. The materiel control section will maintain a current ASL listing for all supported commodities, process receipts and requests for issues and turn-ins, provide material release instructions to the warehouse section.

3-22. The section will establish a facility for supported commodities, performing receipt, storage and issue of all supported commodities. It will coordinate with support operations for delivery and pickup of issued assets and turn-ins for maintenance and/or disposal. This includes performing storage and inventory management activities as directed by stock control.

General Supply Section

3-23. The general supply section receives, stores, and issues Class I, II, III (P), and IV in support to the brigade units. This section breaks down into materiel control and handling section that manages Class II, III (P), and IV and a subsistence section that manages Class I. A separate subsistence element is necessary due to the volume of Class I customer traffic. It receives and issues Class I at the field ration issue point through distribution to the FSCs ICW the transportation platoon. The general supply section also receives inoperable equipment and coordinates transportation for the retrograde of equipment out of the AO.

3-24. The distribution company of the BSB delivers configured loads to the individual field feeding sections. The subsistence section varies between the different BSBs with the IBCT BSBs having the more robust section with four personnel, the Fires BDE BSBs having two and the remaining BSBs having three personnel.

3-25. The Class IX supply section provides Class IX to the Field Maintenance Company. This section receives, stores, and issues Class IX, maintains the brigade authorized stockage list (ASL), and provides direct exchange for reparable/salvage items.

ATHP Section

3-26. The ATHP is operated by the supply support platoon's ATHP section. The ATHP section receives, stores, issues, inspects, and performs munitions maintenance support to the BCT. The trucks and equipment in the ATHPs are similar, personnel strength in the HBCT ATHP sections increase by two and the Fires BDE decreases by one. The section receives mission guidance from the BAO in response to command priorities.

3-27. The ATHP section is responsible for establish the ATHP, transloading munitions to BSB resupply transportation assets, positioning battalion ammunition set configurations. The section will also conduct vehicle inspections, conduct limited munitions maintenance operations, provide limited stock configuration based on operational requirements or suspension notices and keep the BAO informed through daily reports ensuring ATHP operations comply with BCT SOPs.

3-28. The section chief will supervise operations ensuring operational safety and keep the BAO advised of operational problems that might affect support capability. During major combat operations (MCO), the ATHP section keeps type and quantity records of munitions at the ATHP. Paperwork received from users or resupply elements are passed along to the BAO as are reports on damaged munitions through communication channels.

ATHP Site Location and Layout

3-29. The ATHP must be properly located to support munitions operations. The site should be located near MSRs and established on firm ground with good drainage and easy access (such as a loop that allows for one-way traffic). Normally, the site should be located within a base cluster, at least 180 meters away from other unit configurations for explosive safety reasons. When determining the ATHP site, security requirements should be established. No standard configuration exists for an ATHP layout. The ATHP should be large enough to maneuver, permit efficient transloading of munitions, and allow limited storage. The BAO should be consulted on site location, layout and munitions-related technical information. DA Pam 385-64 explains Army safety criteria and standards for ammunition and explosives.

FUEL AND WATER PLATOON

3-30. The fuel and water platoon headquarters provides command, control, and supervision of the fuel and water platoon. Additionally, it provides quality control for fuels being dispensed by the platoon. The platoons' water section purifies, stores, and distributes bulk water for the brigade. The water section sets up and operates the water distribution point in the BSA. The distribution platoon provides vehicles and personnel for delivery of water and Class III (bulk) forward to the FSCs and maneuver units.

Water Support Operations

3-31. Modular water operations are characterized by greater self-reliance of maneuver units due to improved forward mobile storage and distribution within the brigade, organic water purification in the brigade, and tailorable, capable logistics organizations. This added water generation capability, along with fewer echelons and mobility improvements eliminate traditional supply point operations and replace it with distribution based operations for enhanced integration of logistics into the operational battle rhythm.

Water Distribution/Storage Operations

3-32. Units will deploy with three combat loads. Water will be re-supplied via LOGPACs. The BCT can be expected to obtain bulk water or commercial bottled water in the theater of operations. The type of water obtained is highly dependent on the type of operation being conducted and the overall status/maturity of the theater. During early portions of an operation, the BCT should expect to receive bulk purified water which normally transitions into bottled water during later periods of the operation. To ensure the BSB has a suitable source of water, the BCT TOC must include the identification and location of a water source in its planning. Location of that water source is critical to sustainment of the BCT. Water purification and distribution personnel and equipment are embedded in the BSB distribution company to support the BCT. The BSB distribution company will provide one combat load in 2000 gal capacity containers mounted on HEMMT-LHS pulling PLS trailers during resupply operations.

3-33. The fuel and water platoon in the BSB distribution company operates one water point and provides storage and distribution up to 30K GPD using the Tactical Water Purification System (TWPS). The TWPS in the water purification section is capable of purifying up to 1,500 gallons of water per hour.

3-34. An additional combat load in the FSCs distribution platoon Class III Section will be available as mobile storage in HIPPOs mounted on HEMMT-LHS pulling PLS trailers for resupply operations. There is no water purification capability at the FSC and bulk water is received from the BSB during resupply operations.

3-35. The remaining combat load for the BCT will be at the organizational level, and moved with the unit.

3-36. The BSBs' Supply platoon is capable of handling packaged water for receipt, storage, and issue operations, but requires additional transportation assets for onward movement (packaged water would be treated the same as dry cargo).

Water Purification

3-37. Within the BCT, water purification, storage, and distribution will take place in the BSB distribution company. The BSB has the distribution assets to deliver bulk water forward to the FSC during resupply operations. The FSC will in turn distribute water to the units they support as part of the resupply operations. Bulk water purification will not be conducted forward of the BSB.

3-38. In an arid environment, water sources are limited and widely dispersed. Operations in an arid environment create more demand for storage and distribution capabilities than other climatic conditions. Therefore, operations in arid environments will require a greater commitment of water assets in the sustainment brigade as bulk water will need to be produced at the port, distributed forward and stored at the sustainment organization at EAB. Water units required in an arid environment include modular QM water purification and distribution companies with arid augmentation and additional truck units to support line haul distribution of bulk water forward.

Water Purification Equipment

3-39. Water purification, storage, and delivery equipment continues to be the key to establishing an acceptable distribution velocity for water supply. The Lightweight Water Purifier (LWP) is a means for providing safe drinking water for early entry operations. The LWP can support the daily water consumption requirements for 70-225 personnel. There is one Tactical Water Purification System (TWPS) and two LWPs in the BSB to handle brigade water requirements.

Fuel Section

3-40. The fuel section of the fuel and water platoon receives, stores, and issues bulk petroleum to the BCT. The section is mobile and, with modular tankracks, provides the ability to displace even when loaded with fuel.

3-41. Due to the capabilities and mobility of each type of BCT and support brigade, the BSB fuel section will vary in accordance with equipment and usage differences. Due to unit mobility requirements, the SBCT does not have 5K tankers, whereas the HBCT BSB section has 15 5K tankers. HEMTT tankers vary as well with the HBCT and SBCT BSBs having 14 each, the IBCT BSB having 11 each, and the Fires BDE BSB having 18 each.

3-42. Bulk fuel will be issued based on priorities established by the BCT S-4 with guidance from the BCT commander. The BSB distribution company provides unit distribution to the FSCs, as determined by fuel consumption and distances. The BSB support operations officer is responsible for coordinating the resupply of bulk fuel to the FSCs and the BSB distribution company.

SUMMARY

3-43. The BSB distribution company manages the distribution of supplies to the BCT through the transportation platoon, Class IX warehouse, GSO section, ATHP and Fuel and Water platoon. Without an organic maintenance section, the distribution company relies on the field maintenance company for maintenance support.

This page intentionally left blank.

Chapter 4

Field Maintenance Company

The nature of the modern battlefield demands that the maintenance system that is flexible and responsive, and focused on returning systems to operational status quickly and as near as possible to the point of failure or damage. This requirement implies a forward thrust of maintenance into brigade areas. Maintenance assets move as far forward as the tactical situation permits to return inoperable and damaged equipment to the battle as quickly as possible. Field maintenance accomplishes this mission by isolating faults and replacing failed components. This chapter describes the mission, organization, and operations of the field maintenance company (FMC).

SECTION I – MISSION

4-1. The mission of the FMC is to provide field level maintenance support for the BCT or support brigade. This unit is employed in the brigade support area (BSA) and operates as part of the BSB. This unit provides field maintenance support to units in the BSA, technical inspection services, shop stock and bench stock, maintenance management and production control functions. The FMC provides lift capabilities for the repair shops, recovery of organic equipment, recovery to supported units, and support of maintenance evacuation.

SECTION I – ORGANIZATION

4-2. FMCs are tailored to the specific equipment and densities of the BCT they support. Thus, the organizational structure of both personnel and equipment will vary in different BSBs. See Figure 4-1 for an example of one type of FMC.

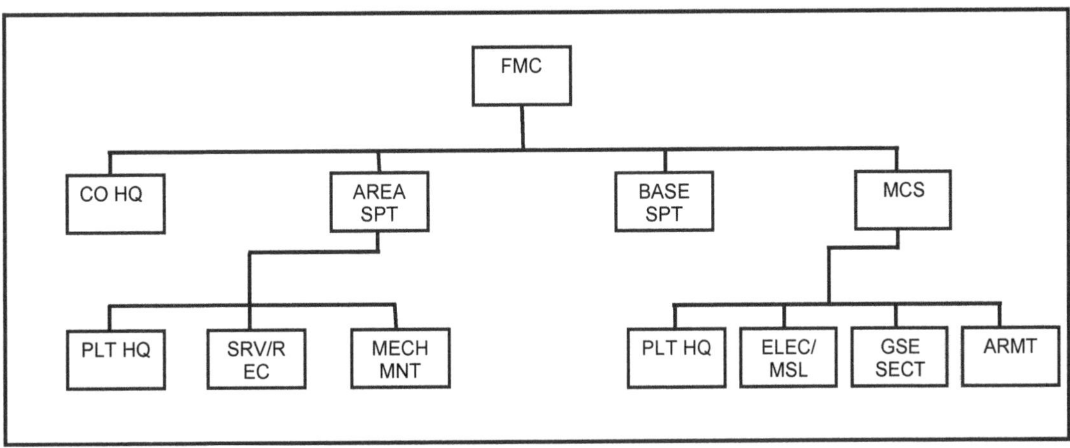

Figure 4-1. The Field Maintenance Company

COMPANY HEADQUARTERS

4-3. The company headquarters section is located in the BSA and provides C2 for all personnel assigned or attached to the company. The headquarters section provides information and advice concerning maintenance operations throughout the BSA to the BSB commander, support operations staff, the BSTB and the brigade headquarters.

Company Commander

4-4. One of the company commander's chief responsibilities is to execute the BCT and BSB commanders' maintenance plans in support of the BCT commander's scheme of maneuver. He manages task organization and employment of all maintenance assets to include combat repair team (CRT) missions and recovery assets. He collaborates and coordinates with the BSB SPO and BCT S4 to determine the best maintenance concept of support and maintains continual communications with higher, lower, and adjacent units.

Executive Officer

4-5. The company XO is the company second in command and the primary internal logistics planner and coordinator. The XO and the company headquarters section serve as the company staff and operate the company CP.

4-6. The company XOs conducts continuous battle tracking, ensures accurate and timely tactical reports are sent to the BSB TOC.

4-7. Other responsibilities include assuming command of the company as required. In conjunction with the 1SG, plan and supervise the company logistics and defense effort before, during, and after the battle. Prepare the company OPORD for the commander. Conduct tactical and logistics coordination with higher, adjacent, and supported units.

4-8. The XO assists the commander in issuing orders to the company, headquarters, and attachments, conduct additional missions as required. These may include serving as OIC for the quartering party, company movement officer, or company training officer and assist the commander in preparations for follow-on missions.

First Sergeant (1SG)

4-9. The first sergeant is the company senior NCO and normally is its most experienced Soldier, assisting the commander in establishing and maintaining discipline. The 1SG is the commander's primary logistics and tactical advisor and is an expert in collective skills. The 1SG helps the commander and XO to plan, coordinate, and supervise all logistics activities that support the company mission. The 1SG operates where the commander directs or where his duties require him.

4-10. The 1SG supervises, inspects, and observes all matters designated by the commander. He collects rollup data for the company LOGSITREPs and PERSITREPs and forward to the battalion administrative and logistics operations center (ALOC). He conducts training and ensures proficiency in individual and collective tasks. The 1SG oversees medical evacuation of sick, injured, and wounded Soldiers to supporting medical treatment facilities and movement of Soldiers killed in action to the supporting mortuary affairs collection point.

SECTION III – OPERATIONS

MAINTENANCE CONTROL PLATOON

4-11. The maintenance control platoon consists of a platoon headquarters, maintenance control section, and a service and recovery section. The headquarters section provides C2, supervision and administrative support for the platoon.

Maintenance Control Section

4-12. Under the direction of the maintenance control officer (MCO) the maintenance control section (MCS) directs, controls and supervises the unit's field maintenance mission and activities. The section provides technical inspection services and maintains a shop stock/bench stock for base shop operations. This section performs maintenance management and production control functions for units operating within the BSA. The MCS is best located in close vicinity of the distribution company's Class IX section. The MCS is the manager for all field maintenance and recovery mission actions within the BSA.

4-13. This section provides the technical inspectors, monitors the maintenance actions, and maintains limited combat spares (shop stock and bench stock). The technical inspectors are responsible for all aspects of quality assurance, technical inspection, and quality control maintenance activities of the company. The MCS provides maintenance management information to the BSB support operations section. If maintenance sections exceed either capabilities or capacities, the MCS can request backup maintenance support through the BSB support operations section from EAB. The MCSs throughout the varying BSBs have identical capabilities. The SBCT FMC MCS has almost double the personnel to manage the FMC's larger role in maintenance operations.

Service and Recovery Section

4-14. The service and recovery section provides welding and lift capabilities for the repair shops, recovery of organic equipment, and recovery support to the distribution company, medical companies and elements in the BSA. To maximize the effectiveness of recovery assets, units will employ self-recovery and like-vehicle recovery techniques as the first option. If the unit or combat repair teams (CRT) is unable to perform the recovery mission, it will report the need for recovery to the MCS. The MCS will dispatch a recovery team to perform recovery operations at the breakdown site. If damage is excessive and a vehicle is unable to be recovered by internal assets, the BSB SPO will coordinate with EAB support elements for recovery support.

Combat Repair Teams (SBCT)

4-15. The SBCT FMC has five CRTs that are dispatched to the forward locations of the infantry battalions, RSTA squadron, and FA battalion to conduct field maintenance. The CRTs are controlled by the maintenance control officer who coordinates with the supported battalion S4 and XO to establish work priorities, control movements, and integrate CRT operations into the supported battalion OPLANs. Shop stocks are permitted for each CRT which will remain 100% deployable in the first lift; the CRT may not stock more than they can carry in organic vehicles.

Wheeled Vehicle Repair Platoon/Section (SBCT/Fires BDE)

4-16. The SBCT FMC has a wheeled vehicle repair platoon and the Fires BDE FMC has a wheeled vehicle repair section (which resides in the MCS platoon) that provides the capabilities for automotive repair of wheeled vehicles. The wheeled vehicle repair platoon/section provides field maintenance for the organic wheeled vehicles in the SBCT and all supported units within the BSA. It is managed by the MCS. The wheeled vehicle repair platoon also provides backup maintenance to the forward CRTs. The wheeled vehicle repair platoon /section performs troubleshooting, minor (nonstructural) welding, major and secondary component replacement, wheel assembly, and line replaceable unit (LRU) replacement as part of its replace forward concept.

4-17. The MCS maintains combat spares and uses controlled component substitution and cannibalized spares obtained from non-repairable vehicles. Repair cycle time is expedited and maintenance is simplified by leveraging diagnostics/prognostics technology to identify major component failures and then replace the components. These components include LRUs, major assemblies, and other subcomponents. Vehicles that cannot be repaired, as well as serviceable major components, are recovered to the MCS, where they are further classified and used at the cannibalization point until they can be evacuated out of the BSA or used as Class IX repair parts.

Maintenance Platoon

4-18. The maintenance platoon consists of a platoon headquarters section, field maintenance section, a ground support equipment repair section; missile/electronics repair section and an armament section. The SBCT FMC does not contain a maintenance platoon.

Field Maintenance Section (HBCT/IBCT)

4-19. The field maintenance section provides base shop and on-site field maintenance on wheel and track vehicles.

Ground Support Equipment (GSE) Repair Section

4-20. The GSE section provides field maintenance on non-vehicular environmental control, power generation, water purification, POL, CBRN, and engineer equipment to the BCT headquarters, the BSTB, the BSB and, on an area basis, for units operating in the BSA. The GSE repair section provides back-up field maintenance support for BCT elements as required. Within the MEB these functions are performed by an electronic equipment maintenance platoon.

Missile/Electronics Repair Section

4-21. The missile/electronics repair section provides field maintenance to the brigade's missile and electronic equipment/weapon systems for those battalions that don't have the capability in FSCs. It conducts float management of communications equipment and other electronic items to the FSCs. The section centralizes and consolidates military intelligence (MI) and signal repairs for brigade troops and units not having embedded capabilities in FSCs and provides back-up field maintenance support for BCT elements.

Armament Section

4-22. The armament section provides field maintenance for weapons assigned to the BSTB, BCT HQs, BSB, and, on an area basis, for units operating in the BSA. The armament section provides consolidated low density equipment armament support to the BCTs units as required.

FIELD MAINTENANCE OPERATIONS

Two-Level Maintenance

4-23. Field maintenance is repair and return to user, and is generally characterized by on (or near) system maintenance, often using line replaceable unit and component replacement, battle damage assessment, repair and recovery. Field level maintenance is not limited to remove and replace, but also provides adjustment, alignment, service and fault/failure diagnoses. Field maintenance is performed at all levels of the Army and most units have at least some organic field level maintenance capability. Sustainment maintenance is characterized by "off system" component repair and/or "repair and return to supply system" and can be employed at any point in the integrated logistics chain. Figure 4-2 shows the decision process between the two levels of maintenance.

4-24. Sustainment maintenance, which is provided at echelons above brigade, focuses on repairing components, assemblies, modules, and end items in support of the distribution system. The intent of this level of maintenance is to perform off-system repairs on all supported items to a standard that provides a consistent and measurable level of reliability. The component is retrograded to a sustainment maintenance repair activity through the distribution system. Once the repair is completed, the component is returned to the distribution system as a serviceable asset.

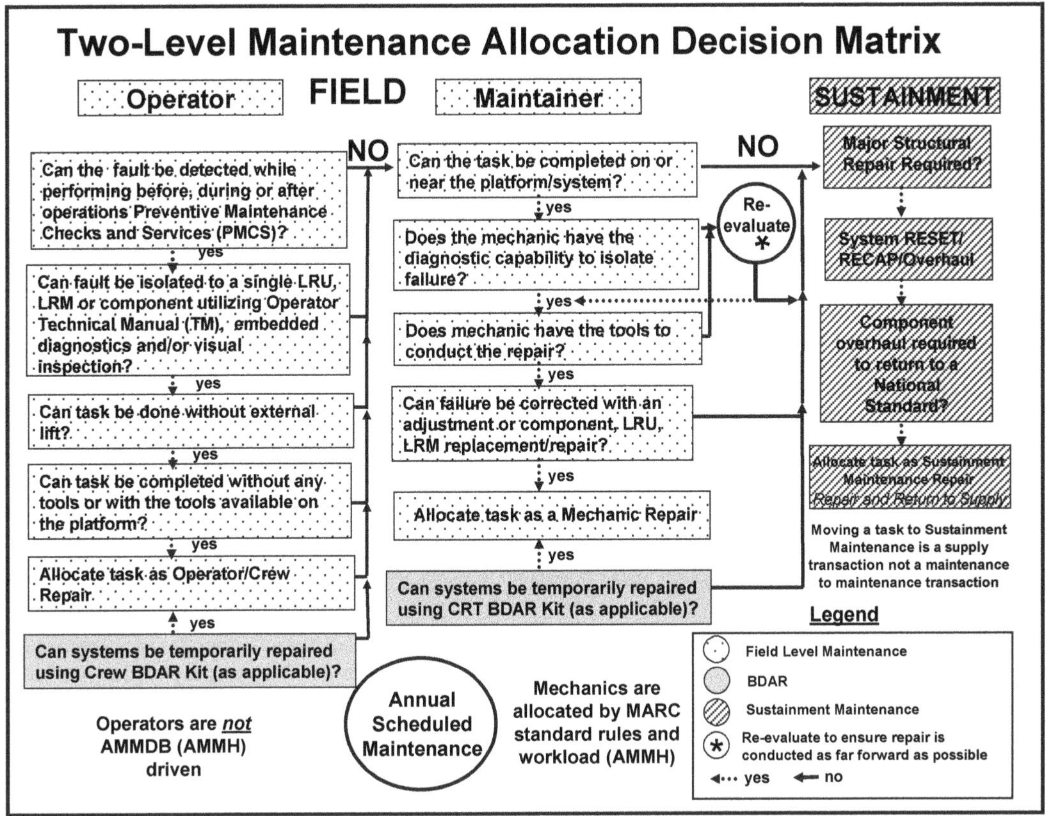

Figure 4-2. Two Level Maintenance Matrix

Replace Forward/Repair Rear

4-25. With replace forward/repair rear doctrine, the FMC uses field maintenance that quickly returns systems to a mission capable or fully mission capable status. Faults that do not render a system non-mission capable (NMC) will be deferred until augmentation arrives or the operational pace permits more repair time. To be most efficient and to generate combat power, the FMC will often focus on the replacement of LRUs and major assemblies, but, when appropriate, may perform on-system repairs of components. The majority of the FMC assets are located in the BSA to reduce the burden placed on maneuver elements. In the SBCT, the CRTs will carry a minimal Class IX load. Due to its limited size, the CRT will often require a daily resupply of mission critical repair parts.

4-26. Equipment that is beyond the FMC/CRT capability will be evacuated to the BSA (in the SBCT), evacuated beyond the BSA, or replaced. Either like-vehicle recovery or FMC recovery assets will perform the evacuation to the BSA. If a vehicle is unable to be recovered to a maintenance collection point (MCP), the BSB SPO will coordinate with EAB for transportation and evacuation assets. There are no set evacuation timelines.

4-27. The BSB SPO may coordinate with EAB maintenance elements for additional resources to assist in restoring combat power. The SPO may coordinate for Class VII replacements which can be either components of end items (COEI) such as radios, night vision devices, or small arms, or end items such as vehicles.

4-28. When NMC equipment is replaced with a Class VII spare, supply sergeants, S4s and property book personnel must be incorporated into the process in order to maintain accountability. Maintenance personnel ensure that Class VII items are operational and either ready for use or installation. Class VII replacements will be delivered by EAB support elements.

Base Maintenance Operations

4-29. The FMC retains a maintenance capability in the BSA since certain pieces of test equipment are not easily transportable. Base maintenance provides dedicated field maintenance on an area basis to the BSB units as well as back-up support to the FSCs, CRTs and supported maneuver battalions. The MCS operates automated maintenance systems to support the BCT companies and the BSB. It also serves as the main collection point for all maintenance records prior to being sent to the BSB SPO staff. Base repair sections can perform contact maintenance missions as required.

Maintenance Management

4-30. Maintenance management in the BCT requires coordination and collaboration between the battalion/brigade S4s and SPOs, CRTs, and the MCO. While battalion S4s and their commanders are accountable for their unit readiness, the MCO provides control, coordination, overall management of maintenance assets and collection for maintenance and readiness data. The SPO tracks maintenance and supply data and trends, provides guidance to the MCO on priorities as they are passed down from the brigade commander, develops current and future support plans, and acts as the central logistics integrator for the BCT and BSB commanders.

4-31. The Army Maintenance Management System (TAMMS) (DA Pam 750-8) describes the forms and records required to perform field level maintenance. The equipment data reports are generated to provide the information needed to plan, manage, and control the equipment. The MCO and MCS use these records to control the maintenance schedules and services, inspections, and repair workloads. Reports are used to report, request, and record repair work. These records help maintain visibility of the status of equipment, equipment uses, and logistics reports. The SOP needs to detail procedures established by the BCT to provide C2 of the equipment.

Controlled Exchange

4-32. Controlled exchange is the removal of serviceable components from unserviceable but economically reparable equipment for immediate reuse in restoring another like item of equipment to combat serviceable condition. The unserviceable component must be used to replace the serviceable component or retained with the end item that provided the serviceable component. Commanders at brigade level will set guidelines for controlled exchange. Controlled exchange is managed by the BSB commander IAW the set priorities and is maintained within the maintenance control section of the BSB. Refer to AR 750-1 for more information on, and regulatory guidelines for, controlled exchange.

Cannibalization

4-33. Cannibalization is the authorized removal of components from materiel designated for disposal. It supplements supply operations by providing assets not readily available through normal supply channels. During combat, commanders may authorize the cannibalization of disabled equipment only to facilitate repair of other equipment for return to combat. Costs to cannibalize and urgency of need are considered in the cannibalization decision. Cannibalization of depot maintenance candidate items, controlled exchange, or component parts by field organizations is prohibited. Exceptions will be made only in urgent cases of field operational readiness requirements and then only with the written concurrence of the AMC major subordinate command. Cannibalization is not authorized during peacetime without approval from the national inventory control point (NICP). Refer to AR 750-1 and AR 710-2 for more information on cannibalization.

Battle Damage Assessment And Repair (BDAR)

4-34. BDAR is the rapid return of disabled equipment to the force through field-expedient repair of components. BDAR restores minimum essential combat capabilities to support the mission or to enable self-recovery. BDAR is accomplished by bypassing components or safety devices, cannibalizing parts from like or lower priority equipment, fabricating repair parts, taking shortcuts to standard maintenance, and using substitute fluids, materials, or components. Depending on the repairs required and the amount of time available, repairs may or may not return the vehicle to a fully mission capable status. See FM 4-30.31, Recovery and Battle Damage Assessment and Repair, for more information.

Maintenance Planning

4-35. Responsive maintenance support speeds up the return of essential combat systems to battle. Maintenance planning should include the maintenance priorities approved or established by the commander. Maintenance teams dispatched as far forward as possible reduce the requirement to evacuate equipment. The thrust of the maintenance effort is to replace forward and fix rear.

4-36. Planning considerations for maintenance support in offensive operations include rapid repair and return of NMC equipment to support the operation and establishment of command maintenance priorities. Other planning tasks include:

- Identify maintenance collection points that are ideally collocated at or near casualty collection points for mutual security purposes that emphasize BDAR.
- Establish criteria for requesting additional recovery assets.
- Consider the feasibility of splitting recovery assets to provide broader coverage for attacking companies.
- Identify critical combat spares and have them ready to move forward on short notice.
- Ensure rapid repair and return of NMC equipment to support the operation.

4-37. The commander establishes his maintenance priorities based on what systems and units are critical to the success of the operation. Maintenance procedures must place emphasis on BDAR. The BSB can send limited back-up forward to support the FSCs' FMTs' at the maintenance collection point (MCP) to ensure support is positioned well forward. Forward supporting maintenance teams from the FMC must have the necessary transportation, communications assets, tools, and repair parts.

4-38. The SPO plans and recommends the allocation of resources in coordination with the supported unit's chain of command. This includes coordination of the maintenance company's operations. He also forecasts and monitors the workload for all equipment by type.

4-39. Customer units will transmit the logistics situation report (LOGSITREP) electronically to the brigade S-4 and BSB SPO. This allows support operations to identify problems quickly and allocate resources more efficiently.

Summary

4-40. The FMC provides a maintenance system that is flexible, responsive, and focused on returning systems to operational status quickly and as near as possible to the point of failure or damage. The FMC accomplishes this by moving forward into brigade areas. Its flexible assets are able to move as far forward as the tactical situation permits in order to return inoperable and damaged equipment to the battle.

This page intentionally left blank.

Chapter 5

Brigade Support Medical Company

The brigade support medical company (BSMC) provides Roles 1 and 2 AHS support to all BCT units operating within the brigade AO. The company also provides Roles 1 and 2 AHS support on an area basis to all BCT units that do not have organic medical assets. The company provides C2 for its organic and attached/OPCON medical augmentation elements. The BSMC locates and establishes its company headquarters and a brigade Role 2 medical treatment facility (MTF) in the BSA. This chapter describes the mission, organization, employment, and operations of the BSMC.

SECTION I – MISSION

5-1. The mission of the BSMC is to provide AHS support to all units operating within the BSA. The BSMC operates a Role 2 medical facility and provides AHS on an area basis to all BCT units that do not have organic medical assets. The BSMC provides C2 for its organic elements and operational control of medical augmentation elements. The BSMC locates and establishes its company headquarters in the BSA and establishes a BSMC Role 2 MTF and, when required, may be augmented with a surgical capability.

SECTION II – ORGANIZATION

5-2. The BSMC is organized into a company headquarters, treatment and evacuation platoons and preventive medicine (PVNTMED) section, a mental health section, a brigade medical supply office (BMSO) section, a medical treatment platoon and an evacuation platoon. The BSMC in the Stryker BCT does not have the BMSO and full MEDLOG support staffing that exists in the other BCTs. The MEDLOG personnel in the Stryker BCT are assigned to the headquarters section of the BSMC. The health services materiel officer, MEDLOG NCO, and the pharmacy NCO normally assigned in a BMSO are not present in the Stryker BCT. However, the Stryker BCT does have a MEDLOG NCO, two MEDLOG specialists, and one biomedical equipment specialist assigned to the headquarters section of the BSMC and is expected to provide the same level of MEDLOG support as outlined above. A typical BSMC organization is shown in Figure 5-1.

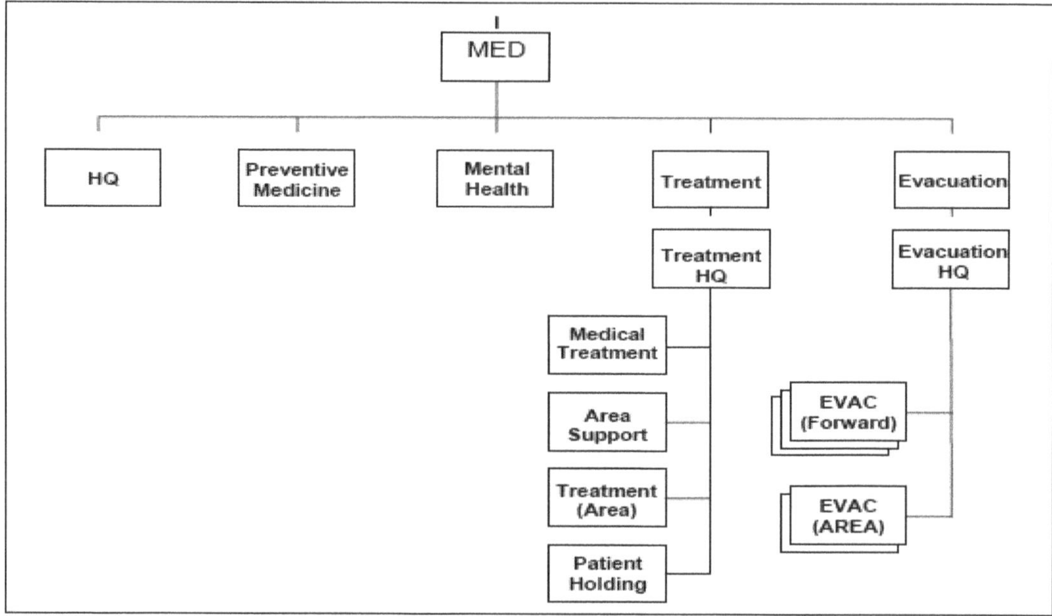

Figure 5-1. The Brigade Support Medical Company

SECTION III – OPERATIONS

COMPANY HEADQUARTERS

5-3. The company headquarters section provides C2 for the company and attached units. It provides unit-level administration, general supply, and CBRN operating support. The company also provides emergency medical equipment maintenance for the medical platoons/sections in the BCT.

5-4. The company headquarters section is organized into a command section, a supply section, and an operations section consisting of unit decontamination, CBRN, and a small arms repair capability. The command section is responsible for providing billeting, security, training, administration, and discipline for assigned personnel. This section provides C2 of its assigned and attached personnel.

5-5. The company commander has direct access to the brigade surgeon. He advises the BSB commander on medical aspects of battalion operations and on the health of supported personnel. The company XO is the principal assistant to the company commander on the tactical employment of the company assets. The basic considerations which influence the employment of medical assets within the brigade are dependant on the brigade commander's plan, the anticipated patient load, expected areas of casualty density, and the medical treatment and evacuation resources available.

5-6. The medical company commander ensures that the medical annex of the OPLAN includes procedures to handle and treat CBRN casualties and provision for chemical protective shelter systems and decontamination augmentation. The annex lists provisions for supporting air and ground ambulances, augmentation of medical support assets for contingency operations, and for medical representation on casualty damage assessment sections.

5-7. The medical company, in coordination with the support battalion S-2/S-3, also develops a combat lifesaver program for support battalion personnel. Training is most critical for elements which deploy separately such as FMTs, contact teams, and truck drivers. However, the program covers all elements of the support battalion.

Preventive Medicine

5-8. The preventive medicine section consists of an environmental science officer and a preventive medicine specialist. Commanders are responsible for protecting their Soldiers from disease non-battle injury (DNBI), and must emphasize and enforce high standards of field sanitation and personal hygiene. Preventive medicine measures (PMM) to counter the health threat and prevent DNBI are the most effective, least expensive means of providing commanders with the maximum number of healthy Soldiers. Role 1 of PMM can be found throughout the BCT and Role 2 in the BSMC.

5-9. Role 1 PMM is what the Soldier does to stay healthy and prevent disease. In addition to the individual PMM responsibilities, each company-sized unit is required (AR 40-5) to have a field sanitation team. This team oversees unit PMM and monitors collective PMM tasks such as hand wash stations, removal of wastes and garbage, latrines, food service sanitation, and other general sanitation responsibilities as required.

5-10. Role 2 PMM personnel are in the preventive medicine section of the brigade support medical company (BSMC). These organic specialists monitor PMM, provide training to field sanitation teams, conduct limited pest control activities, and recommend actions to prevent or reduce DNBI within the unit.

5-11. The preventive medicine (PVNTMED) section has primary responsibility for supervising the unit PVNTMED program described in FM 4-02.17. The section is primarily responsible for identifying health threats and occupational/environmental health hazards, assessing the health risk associated with these threats, and recommending protective measures.

5-12. The PVNTMED section provides advice and consultation in the area of health threat assessment, AHS, environmental sanitation, epidemiology, sanitary engineering, and pest management. Through routine surveillance, they identify actual and potential health hazards, recommend corrective measures, and assist in training BCT Soldiers in DNBI prevention programs. For additional information on the operations and function of the PVNTMED section, refer to FM 4-02.17 and DA Pam 40-11.

5-13. PVNTMED activities begin prior to deployment to minimize DNBIs. Actions taken include supporting command awareness of potential health threats and implementing appropriate protective measures, promoting the deployment of a healthy and fit force, coordinating for the performance of an environmental health site assessment (EHSA) and the related environmental baseline survey (EBS), as required.

5-14. Effective PVNTMED operations are characterized by preemptive actions. Lack of or delay in implementing preemptive actions can significantly impact on the deployed force ability to accomplish its assigned mission. Refer to FM 4-02.17, FM 8-250, FM 21-10, and FM 4-25.12 for additional information.

5-15. PVNTMED operations are prioritized based on the mission, health threat, and assessment of data collected through medical surveillance, occupational/environmental health surveillance, pest surveillance, monitoring unit and individual protective measures, inspecting, and reporting observations. Under the oversight of the brigade surgeon, the PVNTMED section monitors and guides implementation of the brigade PVNTMED program.

Behavioral Health

5-16. The behavioral health section/combat and operational stress control (COSC) team is responsible for assisting commanders in controlling combat and operational stress through prevention programs. The COSC team operates under the direction of the BSMC commander and provides brigade-wide behavioral health and COSC services. See FM 4-02.51 for more detail. The behavioral science officer and behavioral health specialist are especially concerned with assisting and training maneuver unit Soldiers and small unit leaders, to include members of UMTs, members of forward deployed medical platoons/sections, and medical treatment personnel of the BSMC.

5-17. This section provides training in the control of stressors, positive combat and operational stress behaviors, and the handling of misconduct stress behavior and combat and operational stress reaction (COSR) in Soldiers. It coordinates COSC training for supported units. The section surveys social and psychological data and advises the command of the findings. It assists and counsels personnel with personal, behavioral, or psychological problems.

5-18. The company behavioral health section uses the BSMC Role 2 MTF as the center for its operations, but is mobile throughout the AO. The section's priority functions are to promote positive stress behaviors, prevent unnecessary evacuations, and coordinate return of Soldiers to duty, not to treat cases. Through the treatment and evacuation platoon leaders and company commander, the section keeps abreast of the tactical situation and plans and projects requirements for COSC support when units are pulled back for rest and recuperation. For definitive information on COSC operations, see FM 6-22.5.

MEDICAL TREATMENT PLATOON

5-19. The medical treatment platoon headquarters consists of a platoon leader and physicians assistant (the medical corps officers in the medical treatment platoon perform their mission at the hospital/clinic during garrison operations), a field medical assistance officer, platoon sergeant, and a patient administration specialist. The treatment platoon operates the Role 2 MTF in the BSA. It also provides assets to reinforce supported unit medical sections. Platoon sections receive, triage, treat, and determine disposition of patients. The treatment platoon in each medical company has a headquarters, medical treatment squads (forward and area), a patient holding squad, and an area support squad.

5-20. The medical treatment section includes two treatment teams to provide Role 1 medical treatment and augmentation support to BCT maneuver battalions, as required. Each of the medical teams has a HMMWV ambulance (with trailer) to transport the team and its equipment. The patient-holding squad provides a patient-holding facility capability of 20 cots. Its primary mission is to hold patients awaiting evacuation from the brigade AO; a secondary mission is to hold Soldiers who are expected to return to duty within 72 hours.

5-21. The medical treatment squad, the area support squad, and the patient-holding squad are the sections required to establish the BSMC Role 2 MTF. Once established, the treatment platoon is responsible for operating the BSMC Role 2 MTF. The BSMC receives, triages, treats, and determines the disposition of patients based upon their medical condition. The medical treatment platoon provides professional services in the areas of sick call services, emergency medical treatment, advanced trauma management, and operational dental care. In addition, it provides basic diagnostic laboratory (blood cell counts, urinalysis, and microbiology for diagnosis) and radiological services and patient-holding support. When patients are able to return to duty after having received treatment, the BSMC Role 2 MTF coordinates with the brigade S1, who in turn contacts the respective unit to pick up the Soldier or follow the brigade SOP. The treatment platoon also serves as the alternate CP for the BSMC.

Treatment Platoon Headquarters

5-22. The platoon headquarters is the command and control section of the platoon. It directs, coordinates, and supervises platoon operations based on the BCT AHS plan directing the activities of the BSMC Role 2 MTF and monitors Class VIII supplies, blood usage, and inventory levels, and keeps the commander informed of critical Class VIII and blood requirements. The headquarters section is responsible for overseeing platoon operations, OPSEC, communications, administration, organizational training, supply, transportation, patient accountability and statistical reporting functions, and coordination with the BSB SPO for patient evacuation.

MEDICAL TREATMENT SECTION

5-23. The medical treatment section consists of two squads, an area medical treatment squad and a forward medical treatment squad. Its personnel work in the Role 2 MTF which provides emergency and routine sick call treatment to Soldiers within the BSA. The forward medical treatment squad is capable of operating independently for limited periods of time to provide advanced trauma management and sick call, as required. The medical treatment squad consists of a field surgeon, physician assistant, health care NCOs and specialists. The area medical treatment squad is identical to the medical treatment squad however more experienced personnel will generally be assigned here.

5-24. The section provides emergency and routine sick call treatment to Soldiers assigned or attached to supported units. When positioned with the BSMC, the treatment section personnel work in the Role 2 MTF. The forward medical treatment squad must be prepared for short notice forward deployment; therefore, personnel, medical equipment sets, and vehicles must be in a state of readiness.

AREA SUPPORT SQUAD

5-25. There are four different sections in the Area Support Squad consisting of the dental section, the physical therapy (PT) section, the laboratory section, and the radiology section. The squad includes a dentist, dental specialist, physical therapist, physical therapy specialist, medical laboratory NCO, medical laboratory specialist, and radiology specialist.

Dental Section

5-26. The dental section provides operational dental care which consists of emergency dental care and essential dental care intended to intercept dental emergencies. This also includes dental consultation and x-ray services. Operational dental care is the care given for the relief of pain, elimination of acute infection, control of life-threatening oral conditions (hemorrhage, cellulitis, or respiratory difficulty); treatment of trauma to teeth, jaws, and associated facial structures is considered emergency care. It is the most austere type of care and is available to Soldiers engaged in tactical operations. Essential care includes dental treatment necessary for prevention of lost duty time and preservation of fighting strength.

Physical Therapy

5-27. The physical therapy (PT) section plans and supervises PT programs through patient self-referral or referral from a medical or dental officer or other health professionals in medical settings. Serve as consultant to commanders, providing guidance within the areas of physical fitness, physical training and injury prevention. It primarily evaluates and treats disorders of human motion through the use of physical/chemical therapeutic means.

Laboratory

5-28. The laboratory section performs clinical laboratory and blood banking procedures to aid physicians and physician's assistants (PAs) in the diagnosis, treatment, and prevention of diseases. Laboratory functions include performing laboratory procedures consistent with the Role 2 treatment capabilities.

Radiology

5-29. The radiology section provides x-ray equipment consistent with the Role 2 treatment capabilities. It is capable of both plain film and regional digital radiography. This section will also have a reach telemedicine capability to request and acquire digital radiographic diagnostic assistance. The section performs routine clinical radiological procedures to aid physicians and PAs in the diagnosis and treatment of patients.

5-30. Along with the area support squad, the medical treatment squad and the patient-holding squad, form the BSMC Role 2 MTF. The area medical treatment squad is the base medical treatment section of the BSMC Role 2 MTF and does not forward deploy. The squad provides routine sick call services and initial resuscitative treatment for supported units.

Patient-Holding Squad

5-31. The patient-holding squad operates the patient-holding facility of the BSMC Role 2 MTF. The holding facility's primary mission is to hold patients awaiting evacuation; a secondary mission is to hold patients who are expected to return to duty within 72 hours. It is staffed and equipped to provide care for up to 20 patients. The patient holding squad consists of the medical surgical nurse, health care NCO, and health care specialists.

5-32. The medical-surgical nurse assigned to the patient-holding squad provides nursing care supervision and is responsible for the operation of the holding facility. Role 2 facilities do not have an admission capability therefore patients held at this facility are not counted as hospital admissions. In addition, the patient-holding facility serves as a patient-overflow recovery area for the forward surgical team (FST).

THE EVACUATION PLATOON

5-33. The evacuation platoon performs ground evacuation and en route patient care for the supported units. The evacuation platoon consists of a platoon headquarters, an area support evacuation section, and a forward evacuation section. The evacuation platoon headquarters element provides C2 for evacuation platoon operations. It consists of platoon leader and platoon sergeant.

Evacuation Platoon Headquarters

5-34. The evacuation platoon headquarters section provides C2 for evacuation platoon operations. It maintains communications to direct ground evacuation of patients. It provides ground ambulance evacuation support for the maneuver battalions of the BCT. It also provides ground evacuation support to other units receiving area medical support from the BSMC. Further medical evacuation to Role 3 hospitals is the responsibility of the supporting air ambulance company and EAB ground ambulance company when in support of the brigade.

5-35. The evacuation platoon headquarters section directs and coordinates ground evacuation of patients. This section supervises the platoon and plans for its employment. It establishes and maintains contact with supported units and forward deployed treatment squads/teams of the BSMC. The platoon headquarters section performs route reconnaissance and develops and issues all necessary route and navigational information, to include graphic control measures, and relays all essential information to its evacuation teams. The platoon headquarters and its evacuation teams communicate on the tactical internet and employ the FBCB2 to receive evacuation requests from supported units. The platoon headquarters also coordinates and establishes ambulance exchange points (AXPs) for both air and ground ambulances, as required.

Evacuation Squads

5-36. The evacuation squads provide ground ambulance evacuation of patients from the BSA and forward areas to the BSMC Role 2 MTF. Evacuation squad personnel perform EMT, evacuate patients, and provide for their continued care en route. Evacuation squad personnel provide the medical treatment that is necessary to prepare patients for movement, provide en route care and maintain supply levels for the ambulance medical equipment sets. They ensure that appropriate property exchanges of medical items (such as litters and blankets) are made at sending and receiving Role 2 MTFs. Each forward evacuation squad consists of six armored personnel carriers (APCs) and the support personnel to man each APC. Each area evacuation squad consists of four each four litter armored truck ambulances and the support personnel to man each ambulance.

Brigade Medical Supply Office

5-37. The BMSO is an informal supply support activity (SSA) and serves as a forward distribution point (FDP) to distribute Class VIII and synchronizes MEDLOG support for medical equipment and its maintenance within the BCT. The BMSO deploys with a three day basic load and preplans resupply sets for the next seven days. These resupply sets will be brought in and maintained by the BMSO for resupply of the BCT as required.

5-38. The BMSO will also have limited ASL "critical" line items to support BMSC Role 2 medical elements and maneuver medical platoon Role 1 requirements of the BCT. This ASL is a basic load of Class VIII supply for the BCT managed as a safety level and released to support the brigade when routine replenishment fails to meet mission requirements or wait times. Upon arrival in theater, the BMSO will be resupplied by push-packages until line item requisitioning is available. Once the automated ordering system is implemented, the BMSO will immediately start requisitioning for replacement of consumed line items using their automated ordering system and Defense Medical Logistics Standard Support (DMLSS) Customer Assistance Module (DCAM). These orders will be routed to the lowest level SSA supporting them in the theater.

5-39. Critical line items are filled from the ASL maintained by the BMSO where the CWT exceeds mission requirements and immediate resupply to the unit is required. The BMSO uses DCAM to create replenishment orders. Routine ordering procedures that support the unit in garrison via DCAM and in effect prior to deployment will resume upon arrival in theater as soon as NIPRNET connectivity is established. Upon receipt of a requisition, the supporting SSA will fill and package the items for distribution to the requesting unit. The BMSO will receive and account for materiel upon arrival to the distribution control point located in the BSA. It will then integrate materiel marked for maneuver Role 1 MTF/BAS with other critical Class VIII supplies and nonmedical items to be forwarded using a common battlefield distribution to the battalions. This materiel will be broken down by classes of supply, and Class VIII packaged material will be delivered to the medical platoons/sections' operating Role 1 MTF/BAS where the medical platoon will inventory the received items and close out the order in DCAM.

5-40. During the initial employment phase, the BSMC may receive configured push packages every three days from the supporting MEDLOG company. During early entry operations, supported medical units/elements operate from planned, prescribed loads and from existing Army pre-positioned stocks identified in applicable logistics plans. Initial resupply efforts may consist of preconfigured medical supply (MEDSUP) packages tailored to meet specific mission requirements. Anticipatory logistics will allow for preconfigured push packages which are shipped directly from CONUS to the BSMC until replenishment line-item requisitioning is established. While resupply by configured packages is intended to provide support during early entry operations and may continue through the initial phase, continuation on an as-required basis may be dictated by operational needs, and according to casualty estimates.

Summary

5-41. The BSMC provides Role 2 AHS support to all BCT units operating within the brigade AO. The company also provides Role 1 and 2 support on an area basis to all BCT units that do not have organic medical assets. The company provides C2 for its organic and attached/OPCON medical augmentation elements. The BSMC locates and establishes its company headquarters and a brigade Role 2 medical treatment facility (MTF) in the BSA.

This page intentionally left blank.

Chapter 6

Forward Support Companies

Forward support companies (FSCs) are organic units of the BSB. FSCs provide field feeding, fuel, ammunition, field maintenance, and distribution support for a combat arms battalion. While normally under the command of the BSB, an FSC may be placed in either a command or support relationship with its supported battalion. Command relationships, such as OPCON or TACON, are generally limited in duration and focused on the completion of a particular task or mission (e.g. the movement phase of an operation). This chapter describes the FMC mission, organization, and operations, and the roles and responsibilities of key leaders and sections. It also describes FSC differences in the various types of BCT FSCs, e.g., infantry, field artillery, cavalry, maneuver, and Battlefield Surveillance Brigade (BFSB) BSC.

SECTION I – MISSION

6-1. The mission of the FSC is to provide direct and habitual logistics support to the supported battalion. An FSC provides field feeding, water, bulk fuel, general supply, ammunition, and field maintenance. The FSC provides each maneuver battalion commander with dedicated logistics assets organized specifically to meet his battalion's requirements. The FSC commander receives technical logistics oversight from the BSB commander. Due to the early entry and fast paced missions, there are no FSCs in the Stryker Brigade Combat Teams BSB.

SECTION II – ORGANIZATION

6-2. The forward support companies in the various BCTs are structured similarly with the most significant differences in the maintenance sections. The maintenance sections vary based upon the equipment and major weapon systems of the supported battalion. The other more noticeable difference is that the airborne IBCTs have a transportation section in their distribution platoons for the movement of infantry Soldiers.

6-3. The FSCs have a headquarters section, field feeding section, distribution platoon, and a maintenance platoon. The distribution platoon consists of a platoon headquarters, Class III section, general supply section, and a Class V section. The maintenance platoon consists of a platoon headquarters, maintenance control section, maintenance section, service and recovery section and the field maintenance teams (FMTs).

6-4. Although the BFSB Brigade Support Company is not part of a BSB, its supply distribution (to include bulk Class III and water), maintenance, and field feeding roles and responsibilities are similar to that of the BCT FSCs. However, The BFSB BSC does not have a Class V distribution section.

SECTION III – OPERATIONS

COMPANY HEADQUARTERS

6-5. The commander must know the capabilities and limitations of the company's personnel and equipment in performing the sustainment mission as well as those of the logistics elements attached to him. His responsibilities include leadership, discipline, tactical employment, training, administration, personnel management, supply, maintenance, communications, and sustainment activities of the company. The FSC commander is responsible for executing the sustainment plan in accordance with the supported battalion commander's guidance. The BSB provides technical oversight to each FSC.

6-6. The FSC commander is the senior logistician at battalion level for the combat arms battalion for general supply, distribution, and maintenance. The FSC commander assists the battalion S-4 with the battalion logistics planning and is responsible for executing the logistics plan in accordance with the supported battalion commander guidance. The FSC is organic to the BSB in BCTs. In Combat Support BDES, the FSC is organic to one of the support CS BDE BNs. In either instance, the FSC may be placed in a variety of command or support relationships within the battalion that it supports.

6-7. The FSC is as mobile as the unit it supports. This mobility provides greater flexibility for the supported commander. The FSC locates within 4 to 14 kilometers from their combat arms battalion support area. The location of the FSC is the supported battalion commander's decision, unless directed otherwise by the BCT commander.

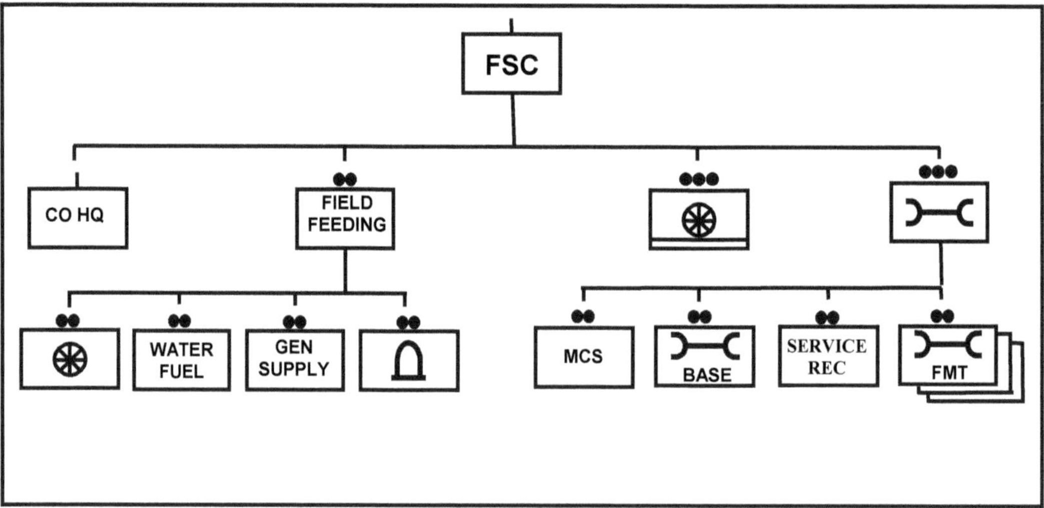

Figure 6-1. The Forward Support Company

6-8. The FSC commander/XO typically collocates with the supported battalion S-1/S-4 at the combat trains command post (CTCP). The battalion S-4 ensures the battalion's orders and requirements are passed to the FSC commander, who has supported the battalion S-1/4 with requisite information during the planning process. One scenario for major combat operations is for the CTCP to be located within the FSC forward location, one to four kilometers behind the battalion (combat trains).

6-9. The FSC is organized for the combined arms, fires battalion and the reconnaissance squadron. (See Figure 6-1) The FSC depends upon the maneuver battalion/squadron and other units for the following support:

- Human resources support.
- Religious support.
- BSB support operations section for a COP for logistics outside the FSC's.
- Maneuver battalion S-2 for intelligence.
- The BSB or EAB for resupply assets to maintain the required quantity of materiel for push forward to the supported battalion.
- The BSMC provides Roles 1 and 2 AHS support. The maneuver battalion provides Role 1 medical support to their FSC.
- The BSB Distribution Company for water distribution to the FSC and its maneuver battalion.

FIELD FEEDING SECTION

6-10. Class I is provided by the food service section. This section provides food service and food preparation for the battalion and organic personnel. It distributes prepackaged and/or prepared food. The food service section has the ability to prepare one heat-and-serve meal and one cook-prepared meal per day.

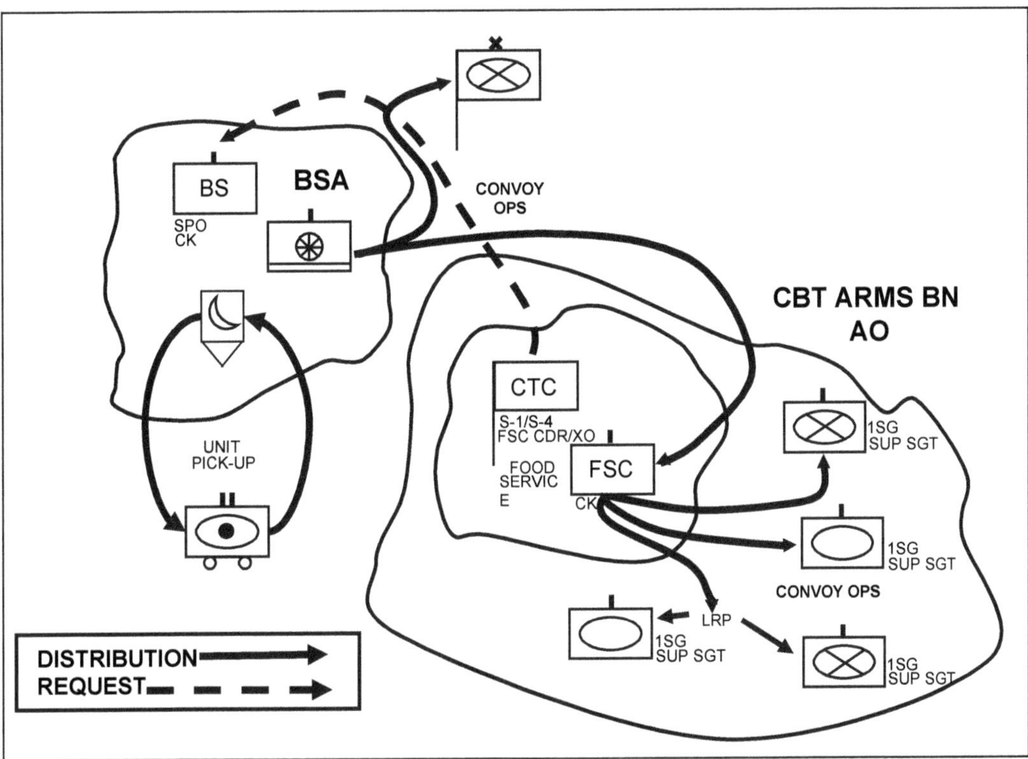

Figure 6-2. Class I Operations

6-11. The field feeding sections reside in the HQ platoon of the FSC. The section has the capability to prepare, serve and distribute the full range of operational rations. They are currently equipped in the same manner as the field feeding section of the BSB, with the containerized kitchen (CK) as the primary field kitchen and one food sanitation center per primary field kitchen. See Figure 6-2.

DISTRIBUTION PLATOON

6-12. The distribution platoon consists of the platoon headquarters, Class III section, general supply section and the Class V section. Figure 6-3 illustrates general distribution from the BSA to the FSC and forward. The Class III section provides retail Class III bulk fuel distribution to the battalion. The general supply section provides the distribution of classes II, III (P), IV and IX to the supported battalion. The Class V section provides the distribution of ammunition to the supported battalion.

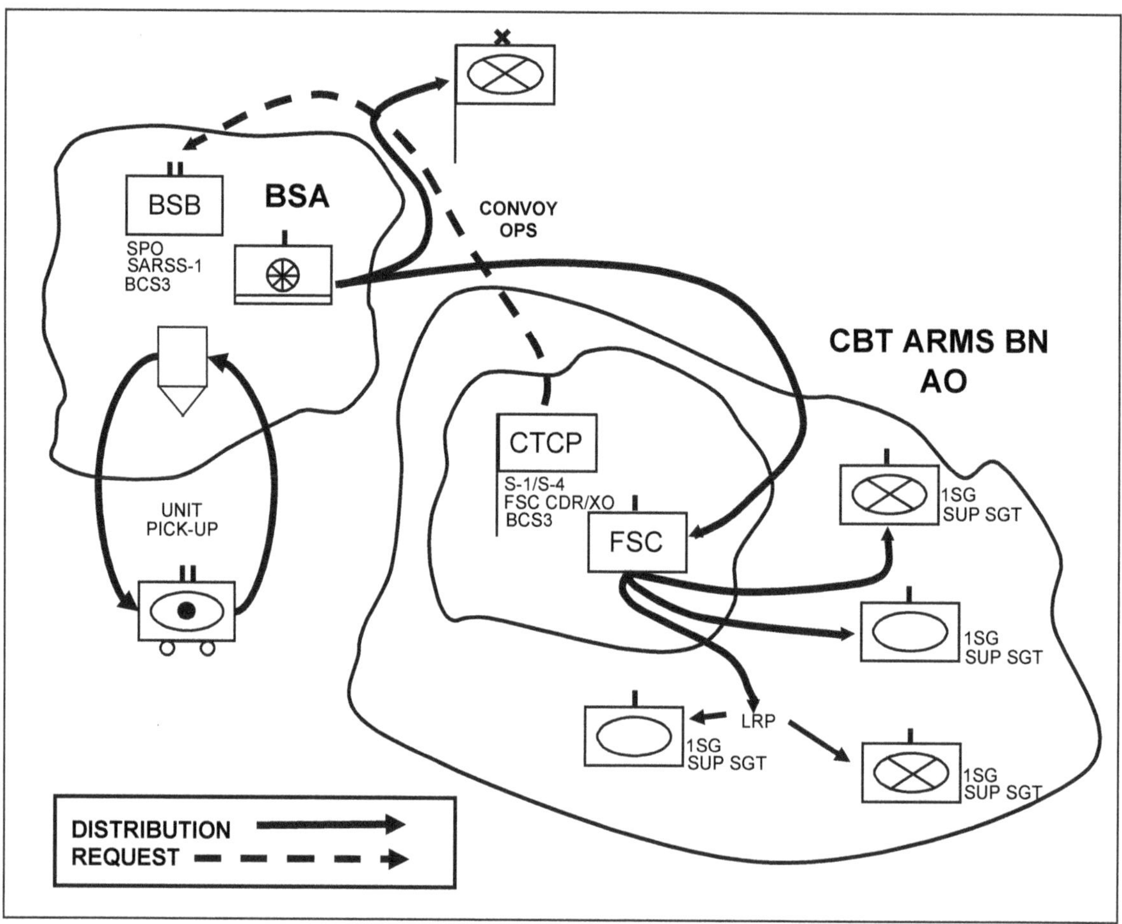

Figure 6-3. General Supply Distribution

6-13. The platoon provides supply and transportation support to the maneuver battalion. The distribution platoon provides Class I, II, III, IV, V, VII, and IX, to the supported battalion. The distribution section has the ability to conduct simultaneous Class III, V retail support to the supported companies.

6-14. The distribution platoon leader provides command and control of the distribution sections of the distribution platoon, manages the distribution of supply Classes II, III, IV, and IX to the battalion, and manages transportation assets of the distribution section, including LOGPAC operations.

6-15. The distribution platoon leader also provides retail Class III (B) and Class V unit distribution to battalion maneuver units and provides order, receipt, and issue capability for Classes II, III (P), IV, and IX.

Platoon Headquarters Section

6-16. The distribution platoon HQ manages the distribution of supplies coming from or passing through the FSC in support of the BCT units.

GENERAL SUPPLY SECTION

6-17. The general supply section is responsible for transporting classes II, III (P), IV, and IX to the supported battalion units coming from or passing through the FSC in support of the BCT units.

Class III Section

6-18. The Class III section conducts replenishment operations for refueling coming from or passing through the FSC in support of the BCT units. The CL III distribution capability of the distribution company pushes fuel to the FSC and loads their HEMTT tankers; the FSC push fuel to the maneuver battalions. See Figure 6-4.

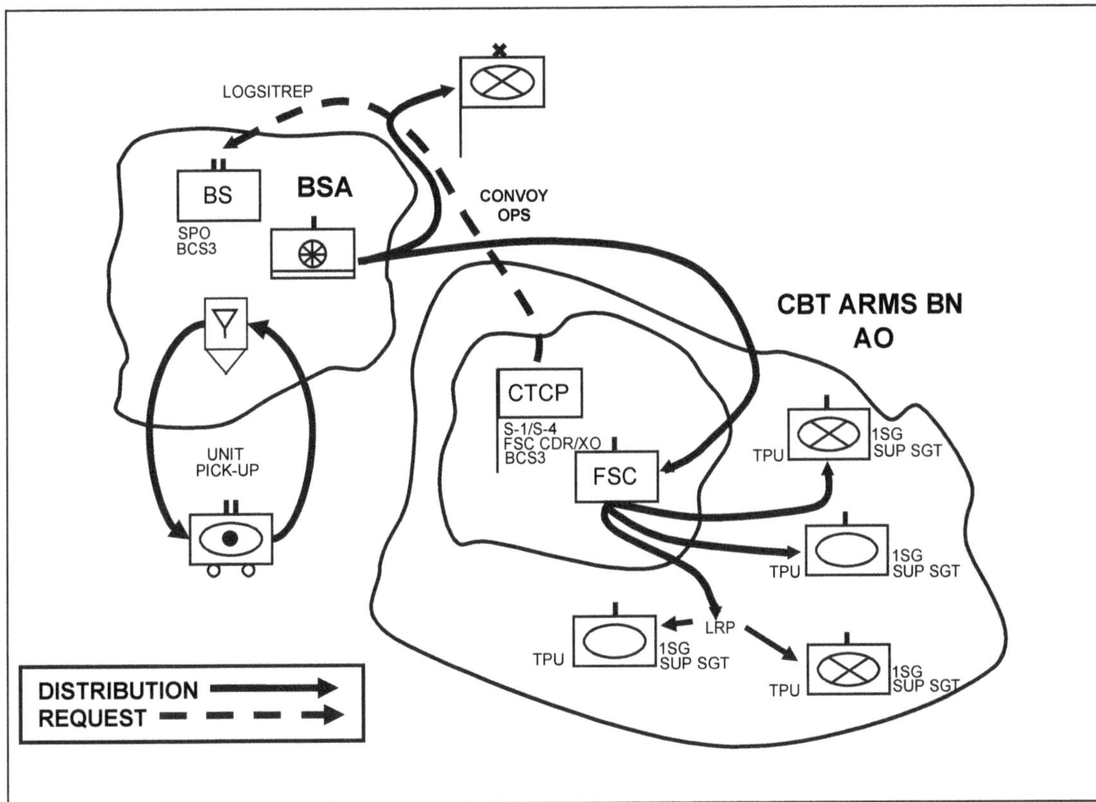

Figure 6-4. Class III Distribution

Class V Section

6-19. The Class V section conducts replenishment operations for ammunition resupply in support of the BCT units. The CL V distribution capability of the distribution company is such that the FSC CL V operation is basically a transloading operation; the distribution company pushes the CL V on a PLS flat rack to the FSC and the FSC pushes it to the maneuver battalion.

MAINTENANCE PLATOON

6-20. The FSC's maintenance platoon provides field maintenance to itself and its supported battalion. The maintenance platoon provides command and control and reinforcing maintenance to the field maintenance teams (FMTs). The FMTs provide field maintenance and battle damage assessment and repair (BDAR) to the maneuver companies. As a maneuver commander task organizes the force, all or part of an FMT goes with the company teams in order to maintain habitual support. The platoon maintains a limited quantity of combat spares (PLL, shop and bench stock) in the MCS. The maintenance platoon's supply section is capable of providing Class IX support (combat spares) to each maneuver company. It also provides exchange of reparable items. The maintenance platoon consists of the platoon headquarters section, maintenance control section, maintenance section, service and recovery section, and the maintenance support teams.

6-21. The maintenance platoon performs all maintenance management functions, dispatching, and scheduled service operations for the maneuver battalion and FSC. The FSC maintenance platoon's priorities are determined by the MCO in coordination by the FSC commander with the supported battalion's chain of command. The platoon performs on-system maintenance. It replaces forward by using diagnostics/prognostics to diagnose major component failure and then replaces that component. These components can include line replaceable units (LRU), major assemblies, or other sub-components. If time, tools, test equipment, and repair parts are available, repairs are done on site. Mechanics perform BDAR IAW applicable technical manuals. As directed, mechanics perform controlled exchange to expedite repairs. The battalion commander is the approval authority for controlled exchange actions and cannibalization is normally in accordance with the BCT commander's policy. The FSC maintenance platoon coordinates backup and pass-back maintenance requirements with the FSC commander.

6-22. During combat, the maintenance platoon's first priority is to reinforce the FMTs mission. The platoon headquarters coordinates with the FSC commander to integrate and support battalion operations. The headquarters section maintains situational understanding of battalion operations. It also maintains FM communications with both the battalion command and logistics nets. This ensures the maintenance platoon maintains asset visibility and tactical situational understanding of logistics.

6-23. Supported battalion units and all other units in the BCT remain responsible for operator and crew level maintenance. Operators/crews may perform BDAR through the use of onboard BDAR kits and will use self-recovery techniques to the greatest extent possible. BDAR kits include tools, bags, supplies, connectors and small parts, and may be configured for both individual maintainers and crews.

6-24. The FSC MCO coordinates the maintenance priorities with the battalion S-4 and MCS. The MCO task organizes the maintenance platoon based on analysis of current and anticipated mission requirements. He is concerned with providing the appropriate support at the unit maintenance control point (MCP) and to the combat companies. The MCP is under the control and is work-loaded by the MCS. It is task organized with the maintenance control section, the maintenance section and the service and recovery section. Task organization of the MCPs maintenance operation is modified based on the MCOs analysis of maintenance requirements, tactical situation. Anything that is not repaired in the MCP, or that is not towed by MCP assets, is recovered to the battalion maintenance section or evacuated to the BSA or EAB.

6-25. The maintenance control section is the management center for all maintenance actions. The FSC's automation systems are collocated in the MCS, the MCO uses them to produce the Army materiel status system (AMSS) readiness reports. The AMSS replaces manual readiness reporting on the front-side of DA Form 2406 (Material Condition Status Report). The maneuver commander is responsible for the operator/crew maintenance functions in his unit. The MCO is responsible for preparing the readiness report for the maneuver commander's signature.

Maintenance Platoon Headquarters Section

6-26. The maintenance platoon headquarters section provides command, control, and supervision for all administrative functions of the platoon. With guidance from higher headquarters, it plans and conducts all necessary training activities.

Maintenance Platoon Leader

6-27. The maintenance platoon leader is responsible for controlling and directing the accomplishment of the platoon's mission. He is responsible to the MCO for ensuring the completion of maintenance jobs and adhering to priority of support as provided. He is responsible for the readiness of the platoon's personnel and equipment. He is also responsible for maintaining the health, welfare, and morale of platoon personnel.

Maintenance Control Section (MCS)

6-28. The MCS is the primary manager for field maintenance in the FSC and supported battalion. The MCS performs maintenance management functions and dispatching operations, and tracks scheduled services for the maneuver battalion and FSC.

6-29. The MCS tracks the calls for support (CFS) and logistics task orders (LTO). The maintenance flow begins when the operator sends a CFS maintenance/recovery request using FBCB2. This message includes the vehicle location and the action requested. The message is sent simultaneously to the 1SG for action and to the FSC support operations section for information.

6-30. When the 1SG receives the CFS from the operator, he sends the LTO to the FMT for action. The FMT responds to the LTO with one of the acknowledgment messages. The operator requesting the maintenance support receives an information copy of the acknowledgment message. When the FMT is unable to provide the necessary support to accomplish the task in the CFS, the 1SG forwards a CFS to the FSC.

6-31. The appropriate section responds to the LTO with one of the acknowledgment messages. Again, the requesting operator receives a copy of the acknowledgment message. When the LTO is accepted, the maintenance section NCOIC responds and sends a mechanic to repair the vehicle. If the mechanic does not have the necessary combat spares on hand, he sends a message to the MCS requesting additional repair parts. If the repair part arrives in a timely manner, the vehicle is repaired on-site or at the UMCP. If the part is not available or has a long order ship time, the vehicle is recovered to the FSC, BSA or EAB as appropriate.

Maintenance Control Officer (MCO)

6-32. The maintenance control officer is the principal assistant to the commander, both battalion and FSC, on all matters pertaining to the field maintenance mission. The MCO serves as maintenance officer for the maneuver battalion and FSC. He is also is the senior person in the UMCP and is responsible for the local security requirements and tying in with adjacent units. He is responsible for managing the maintenance control section, maintenance section, service and recovery section, and the maintenance system teams.

6-33. The maintenance control officer evaluates to ensure the quality of maintenance completed by the maintenance platoon. In conjunction with the platoon sergeant the MCO develops a training and cross-training plan for the maintenance personnel and the maintenance services plan for battalion equipment.

6-34. The MCO manages production control, including assignment of work and compilation of prescribed reports and records. He maintains the commander's maintenance priorities, and anticipates expected workloads, shop progress, repair difficulties, and maintenance supply actions. The MCO coordinates activities of the inspectors and maintenance personnel to ensure adherence to maintenance standards with maneuver battalion S-4 and BSB SPO as appropriate.

Automotive Maintenance Officer

6-35. The automotive maintenance officer provides technical expertise on all aspects of the field maintenance mission. He uses advanced diagnostics and troubleshooting capabilities to isolate system faults and expedite the repair and return of major weapon systems to operation. Due to his expertise, the automotive maintenance officer advises the commander and MCO on all matters pertaining to BDAR.

6-36. The automotive maintenance officer provides input to the FSC and maneuver commanders' plans and organizes resources to execute field maintenance of wheeled vehicles, tracked vehicles, ground support equipment, armament systems, small arms, fire control, and power driven chemical equipment. Further, this officer:

- Evaluates maintenance operations and develops corrective action to comply with regulatory and statutory requirements applicable in garrison and field environments.
- Identifies technical training shortfalls and trains maintenance personnel to accurately diagnose/troubleshoot mechanical, electrical, pneumatic and hydraulic malfunctions using the latest equipment, technical publications, and procedures.
- Provides management, regulatory and technical guidance on establishment of unit stockage of combat spares.
- Provides technical training for automation systems operators and repair parts specialist (92A).
- Assists in ongoing development of the field maintenance SOP as it pertains to field level maintenance operations.
- Oversees unit calibration and Army oil analysis programs and ensures programs are covered in the field maintenance SOP.
- Trains and certifies recovery vehicle operators on safe and correct recovery operations.
- Utilizes automated maintenance management systems to provide maintenance information to the commander and maintenance control officer.
- Assists in the planning, scheduling, and publishing of the scheduled service plan for all assigned equipment.

Recovery Section

6-37. The recovery section provides recovery support to elements of the FSC. This section also provides limited reinforcing recovery support to FMTs. When reinforcing recovery support is required, FMTs send a CFS to the MCS. The MCS then sends a task order to the recovery section to provide backup support to the FMT.

6-38. Vehicles not repairable on site can self recover or be recovered to the UMCP or BSA using a like vehicle. If neither of these recovery options are viable, the crew or operator forwards a call for support (CFS) message to the 1SG. This message includes type of request, action requested, mission, and vehicle location. When FMT recovery assets are not available, the company/team 1SG sends a CFS to the FSC commander. The FSC commander forwards a LTO to the MCS. The MCS forwards the LTO to the recovery section NCOIC. The section NCOIC then acknowledges the LTO.

6-39. If unable to perform the mission, the FSC commander may request assistance through the BSB support operations section by forwarding the original CFS. The BSB support operations section responds to the message by sending an LTO to the recovery section. The recovery section responds with an acknowledgment message. If the BSB recovery section is unable to perform the mission, the BSB support operations section the forwards the original CFS to EAB.

Field Maintenance Teams

6-40. The supported battalion's first level of support comes from the FSC FMTs which are organized to provide field maintenance (organizational and direct support maintenance levels) for all combat platforms organic to maneuver units. The company commander and the MCS set the FMTs priorities IAW the battalion commander's guidance. The FMT operates under the operational control of the maneuver 1SG and is supervised by the FMTs maintenance NCOIC.

6-41. FMTs perform repairs as far forward as possible, returning equipment to the battle quickly. During combat, FMTs perform BDAR, diagnostics, and on-system replacement of line replaceable units (LRUs). Emphasis is placed on troubleshooting, diagnosing malfunctions and fixing the equipment by component replacement. If the tactical situation permits, FMTs focus on completing jobs on site. FMTs carry limited on board combat spares to facilitate repairs forward. If inoperable equipment is not repairable due to a lack of spares, the team uses recovery assets to assist the maneuver company and may recover inoperable equipment to the UMCP or linkup point. FMTs are fully integrated into the maneuver unit's operational plans.

6-42. The MCS gives the FMT a block of work order numbers to track equipment repair. The FMT NCOIC uses the free text message on the CFS to update the MCS on work order status. The FMT opens a job order then sends paper work back to the MCS on parts runs.

SUMMARY

6-43. The FSC provides field feeding, fuel, ammunition, field maintenance, and distribution support for a combat arms battalion. It may be placed in either a command or support relationship with its supported battalion. Command relationships, such as OPCON or TACON, generally being limited in duration and focused on particular tasks or missions. These units are structured accordingly, dependant on the differences between the various types of units (infantry, field artillery, cavalry, and maneuver) it supports.

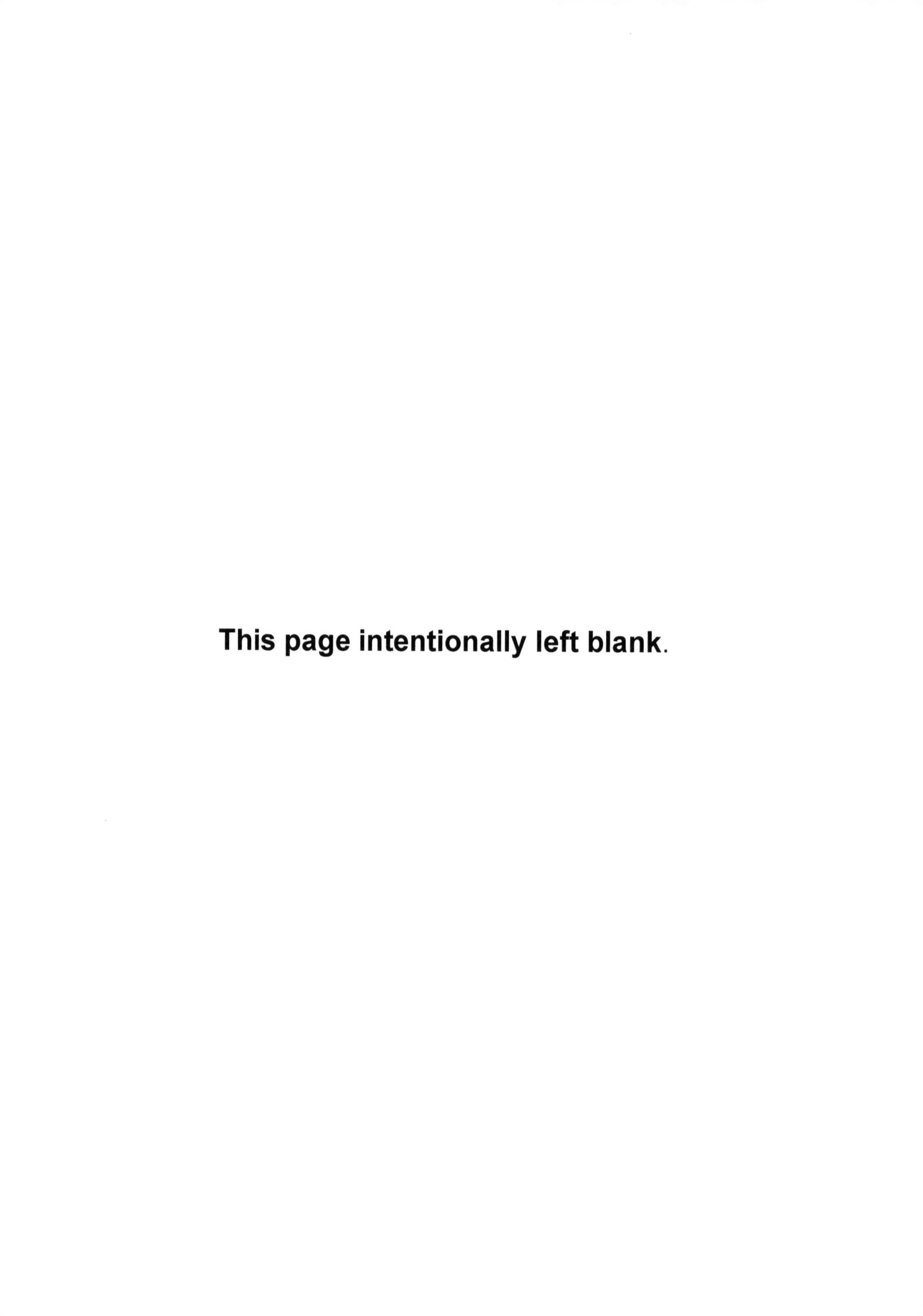

This page intentionally left blank.

Appendix A

Logistics Reporting Tool

A-1. The Logistic Reporting Tool (LRT) is the Army standard for submitting routine logistics status reports from the unit and supply point level. Developed as an independent web-enabled service of the Battle Command Sustainment Support System (BCS3) suite of software, the LRT is intended to augment command and control (C2) data by focusing on the commander's critical sustainment information and/or items of equipment. It provides a snapshot of on-hand stock status, personnel, equipment and projected future requirements. The LRT provides the logistician information from the "bottom-up" with the flexibility to be rolled-up or aggregated at each level of command. The LRT allows users to submit and view reports using the JAVA application, with or without a BCS3 laptop.

A-2. Although UIC-based in reporting structure, the LRT allows creation of unit structure below UIC level if required by mission or specific support situation. The intent is to input the data at the lowest level (e.g. platoon level attachments or supply points), and then project the requirement based on the Logistics Factor Files (LFF) consumption rates and other calculations within the application. Once the data has been published at the national level, the shortages and projected requirements are visible to the next higher command and the support unit at the same time.

A-3. The LRT is not intended as a means of gathering the same information available in a logistics Standard Army Management Information System (STAMIS), nor to serve as the means of requisitioning commodities managed by a logistics STAMIS. The application can accommodate any class of supply, with special emphasis on those classes not managed by a current STAMIS. These classes include Class I, Water, and Class III Bulk.

A-4. Three tools designed to assist in tailoring the application are the Tracked Items List (TIL), the Logistics Factor Files (LFF) and the Unit Task Organization (UTO).

- The TIL function allows the user to identify the list of items to be reported. Once a TIL is created, it can be submitted / published to the network, making it available to all users to access and use for reporting. The list of tracked items can be as small or as large as desired, but sound reporting practices dictate keeping it to the minimum essential items required to meet Commander's and higher echelon reporting requirements.
- The LFF provides automatic calculations on planning cycles, thresholds, feeding cycles and planning days of supply. These planning factors can be automated or user-defined depending on the commanders guidance.
- The UTO function enables each user to run logistics reports against various task organized entities, such as forward operating base (FOB), geographic region, or task force. Proven reporting practices recommend the UTO be developed and published at the highest level possible given the organization or mission. Within sustainment units, it is important to ensure that all supply point entities are included as part of the UTO hierarchy to maintain visibility of all stocks.

A-5. Company level: At company level, a designated individual is responsible for gathering information from the platoon sergeants and publishing a consolidated LRT report for the battalion S4 to view. Regardless of how the data is gathered below the company level, the units with network connectivity can publish the data with the downloaded LRT JAVA application. Pre-formatted EXCEL spreadsheets can be exported /imported from the LRT as an alternative means of submission.

A-6. Battalion level: The battalion S4 is responsible for reviewing reports from all companies and ensuring the reports are complete, timely and accurate. Since the LRT submission is published to the network, there is no need for coordination copies to be forwarded to other entities, such as the brigade support battalion (BSB) support operations. The battalion S4 also has the responsibility for collecting reports from any companies or elements that do not have network connectivity.

A-7. Brigade Combat Team (BCT) level: The brigade S4 is responsible for reviewing reports, rolled up by battalion, FOB or geographical area. The S4 ensures that all reports are complete, timely and accurate. It is recommended that the brigade S4, in coordination with their BSB and the theater's major sustainment units, maintain and update the TIL and UTO for reporting. All changes, including re-supply rates, and updates should be published to the network; and therefore, available to all reporting entities.

A-8. Echelons above Brigade: The LRT process allows for all supporting and supported units to see the individual unit status at the same time. No longer is there a need to collect and forward reports. Changes or corrections can be submitted through follow-up email or a subsequent publication of new information. The process should be more timely and accurate as manual intervention is the exception, not the rule.

A-9. Sample reports from the BCS3 LRT can be found at the following location on the NIPRNET: http://www.cascom.us.army.mil; or by contacting the BCS3 Customer Support Center at https://hd.kc.us.army mil

Appendix B

BSA Layout and Protection

BSA Layout

B-1. The location of the BSA is dependent on terrain features and the geographical location of the supported brigade. Location of EAB logistics units and the battalions' support areas must also be evaluated to ensure that there will be no interruption of throughput. The brigade commander approves the location of the BSA based upon recommendations from the BSB commander and brigade staff.

B-2. The composition of BSA elements will not remain static. The BSB commander must be able to track and control changes. To accomplish this, all ground units entering the brigade area must send a representative to report to the BSB TOC. They will coordinate movement routes, positioning for units locating in the BSA, communications, support requirements and procedures, security responsibilities and arrangements. Guards at entry control points (ECP) going into the BSA will direct representatives of entering units to the TOC. Also, unit commanders will notify the TOC of all support package arrivals and departures. Movement of displaced civilians and local civilians must also be controlled. See Figure B-1 for the layout of a typical BSA.

B-3. Personnel available for defense actions may be extremely limited within certain units. Unit commanders must keep the BSB S2/S3 informed of their situations. The BSB commander will identify a command post as the alternate for the BSA.

B-4. Locations of elements within the BSA will vary depending on METT-TC factors. The BSB commander and S2/S3 must use their best judgment in positioning units. Position the BSB TOC near the center of the BSA perimeter for C2 and security reasons.

B-5. Ensure that units such as the BSB distribution company and the BSB FMC locate their CPs near the BSB's area of operation (closer to the TOC to enhance communications and protection of C2 facilities). Balance the advantages of dispersion (reduced destruction from a single enemy strike) with the disadvantages (C2 constraints and extended perimeter).

B-6. Make supply points accessible to both customers and resupply vehicles and helicopters. Keep Class III points away from other supplies to prevent contamination. They should also be located at least 100 feet from water sources. Locate the MTFs away from likely target areas (ATHP, Class III point, bridges, and road junctions) but near evacuation routes and an open area for landing air ambulances.

B-7. Position the ATHP near, but off the MSR, so that EAB trailers bringing ammunition into the area do not clog up the MSR within the BSA. The ATHP requires sufficient area to perform transload operations without interfering with BSA traffic. Locate the ATHP at least 180 meters from other supplies and 620 meters from the nearest inhabited tent; due to its size, the ATHP will often be outside the BSA. This creates a security issue for the BSB commander that will often require forces from outside the BSA to provide protection. When the ammunition point is sufficiently large, it will be assigned its own area for defense and a security force will be attached.

B-8. Units with heaviest firepower should be positioned along the most threatening avenue of approach.

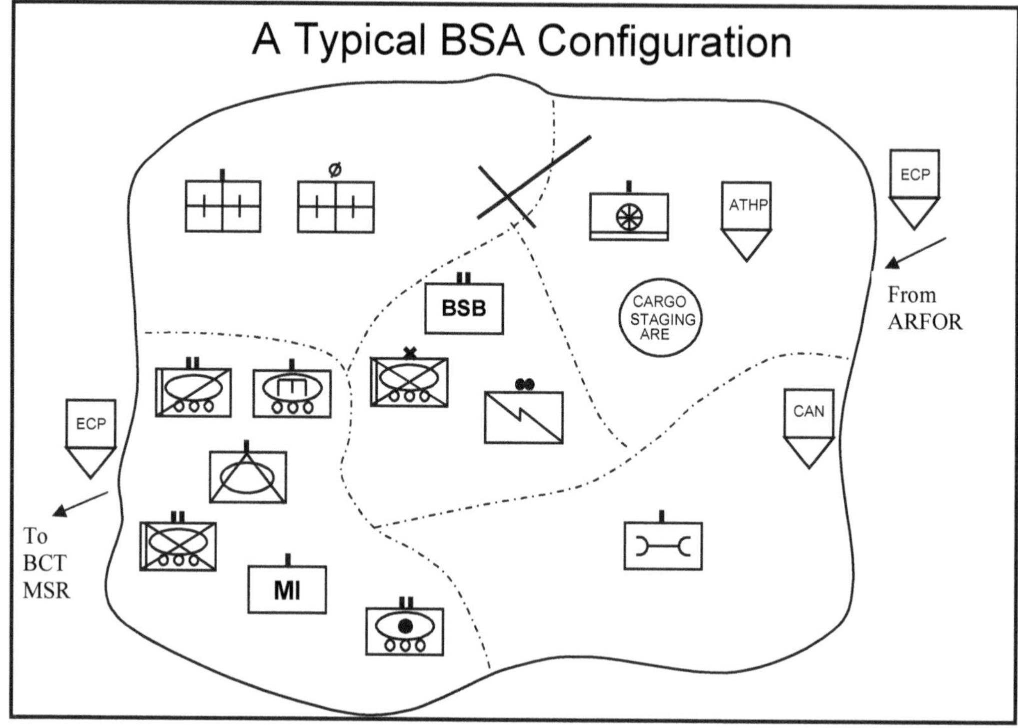

Figure B-1. The Brigade Support Area Typical Layout

BSA Protection

B-9. Tactical logistics organizations are normally the units least capable of self-defense against a large, enemy combat force. Given the common operating environment (COE), they are also often the targets of enemy action. As the enemy threat increases, unit commanders cannot decrease logistics operations in favor of enhancing protection. The supported commander and the logistics unit commander must have previously discussed what risks are reasonable to accept and what risk mitigation measures they should implement based on requirements and priorities including Force Health Protection. Only then can logistics commanders and staffs plan accordingly. Logisticians and unit commanders must be competent in warfighting, military decision-making, maneuver, and other tactical skills to anticipate and decide on appropriate risk mitigation measures.

Commanders Responsibility

B-10. The SBCT commander normally will assign the BSB commander the responsibility for BSA security. The SBCT commander also normally assigns to the BSB commander operational control of all elements located in the BSA in order to accomplish the defense mission. The SBCT commander and the BSB commander must communicate to protect the force and ensure that the units are able to conduct logistics operations.

B-11. The BSB commander's goal is to retain overall freedom of action for fighting military operations. This means—

- The MSRs are clear, unobstructed, and secure.
- Units can move quickly and in an orderly fashion throughout the brigade area.
- Logistics missions and associated activities continue without restriction.
- All logistics units can perform protection operations against a level 1 threat.

B-12. The BSB commander's responsibility for protection extends to convoys and other logistics actions occurring outside of the BSA. LOCs are not necessarily secure for all movements. Commanders and staffs must plan for and coordinate protection for subordinate units and detachments located away from the headquarters.

Perimeter Defense

B-13. The BSB commander organizes a perimeter defense to protect the assigned area or provide security during logistics operations. All elements in or transiting the area assist with forming and defending the perimeter. Based on mission and terrain analyses, the BSB S2/S3 subdivides the area and assigns subordinate and tenant units to those subdivided areas. The S2/S3 receives from subordinate elements the battle position overlay and determines the best protection posture. The perimeter is broken into battle positions of individual, independent positions with interlocking fields of fire. The BSB S2/S3 is responsible for establishing and maintaining the tactical SOP, which will cover as many defense procedures as possible. The shape and size of the defensive perimeter is METT-TC dependent, meaning the perimeter does not necessarily coincide with the boundaries of the area assigned to the BSB. The perimeter shape conforms to the terrain features that best use friendly observation and fields of fire. The commander can increase the effectiveness of the perimeter by tying it into a natural obstacle, such as a river, which allows him/her to concentrate combat power in more threatened areas or operations. The BSB S2/S3 is responsible for providing staff and subordinate commanders with the intelligence update and situational understanding. The BSB S2/S3 is also responsible for intelligence collection planning and management, including patrolling, outside of the perimeter. Intelligence collection management and execution is highly important because, based on collected intelligence, the BSB commander may determine the most probable direction of enemy attack and then weight that part of the perimeter to cover that approach.

B-14. The BSB commander positions his/her forces and plans fire and movement so he or she can respond to the widest possible range of enemy actions. The BSB staff prepares plans, including counterattack plans, which should be rehearsed, evaluated, and revised as needed. The commander coordinates direct and indirect fire plans. Normally, the QRF centrally locates to react to a penetration of the perimeter at any point.

Base Perimeter Defense Planning

B-15. The BSB S2/S3 assigns a perimeter area to each unit in the BSA but should not factor medical units or medical personnel into the perimeter defense plan. The S2/S3 ensures each unit's area of fire mutually supports the adjacent unit's area, when feasible. The S2/S3 coordinates with unit commanders and confirms that units in the BSA have coordinated their boundaries of fire with their adjacent units. The S2/S3 section must synchronize direct and indirect fires, obstacles, patrols, OPs, and sensors to mitigate levels I, II, and III threats use of avenues of approach and infiltration lanes.

B-16. The BSA defense plan must be integrated into the plan for the entire brigade area of operation. This requires that the BSB staff coordinate with the engineer coordinator (ENCOORD) and the brigade S3 for the overall plan. This coordination should include the brigade ENCOORD to ensure integration of engineer support and Class IV materials to harden positions and reduce the effectiveness of enemy weapon systems. The BSB staff must also coordinate directly with staffs of units in areas adjacent to or close to the BSB to plan mutually supporting fires and to prevent firing upon each other. This entire defensive perimeter planning effort must be replicated for protection of logistics elements that operate or move outside of the BSB's specifically assigned area.

B-17. The S2/S3 maintains all defensive plans. The defensive plan shows unit protection responsibilities, locations of mines and obstacles, planned indirect fire coverage, OPs, listening posts (LP), patrol routes, and positions of automatic and anti-armor weapons. The commander may consider using weapon systems that are in the shop for repair if qualified operators are available. If the firing system is operable, these weapons should be included in the BSA defensive scheme, and mechanics should work on them in their fighting positions. Whenever possible, units should occupy the same location within the BSA relative to the other units every time the BSA moves, or units can use several standard configurations for ease of transition. Since night vision devices are not always available, illumination plans must also be included in the overall BSA security plan. In anticipation of the need for QRF or tactical combat forces (TCF), the S2/S3 develops and rehearses procedures to hand-off the battle to arriving QRF, MP response forces, and TCF.

Appendix C

Echelons Above Brigade Logistic Support

SUPPORTING SUSTAINMENT BRIGADE

C-1. All logistics requirements (less medical) beyond the BSB's ability are either furnished by or coordinated through the supporting sustainment brigade. The sustainment brigade supports the BCT on an area basis. When properly task organized, the sustainment brigade is capable of supporting BCT requirements for all classes of supplies (less Class VIII), maintenance, field services, contracting, and other logistics requirements. Through its distribution capability, the sustainment brigade normally provides distribution of supplies to the BSB in support packages. The sustainment brigade operates ATHPs for the distribution of Class V. The sustainment brigade SPO is the POC for BCT logistics requirements above the capacity of the BSB.

C-2. The sustainment brigade is a modular, task-organized unit which will have assigned to it the types and numbers of logistics organizations required to accomplish its assigned mission. Some of the logistics units which may be assigned to the sustainment brigade supporting a BCT and their capabilities are discussed below.

Financial Management Company

C-3. The financial management company provides financial management (financial management operations and resource management) support on an area basis within an AO. FM COs perform the following functions:

- Identifies funding for resource requirements including procurement.
- Makes payments on prepared and certified.
- Provides limited U.S. and non-U.S. pay support.
- Establishes banking relationships and procedures.

C-4. The Sustainment Brigade Financial Management Support Operations Team (FM SPO) monitors and tracks financial management operations throughout the area of operations (AO). The team integrates all FM operations; plans the employment of FM units; coordinates FM requirements. It also coordinates for additional operational and strategic FM support when needed.

Human Resources

C-5. Human resources (HR) companies, platoons, or teams provide area support to the AO using existing structures under the C2 of the STB or CSSB. The HR company, platoons or teams provide:

- Provide postal support to brigades and Military Mail Terminals.
- Track and conduct personnel accountability of personnel who transit the AO.
- Support Theater Gateway Personnel Accountability Team.
- Provide casualty liaison teams at division/corps/theater level and hospital to assist in tracking patients and conducting casualty operations.

C-6. HR support for all brigades and battalions are embedded with the S1. See FM 1-0, HR Support, for specific information on HR operations. HR support beyond the capability of the brigade and battalion S-1 will be requested through the HR Operations Branch within the Sustainment Brigade SPO.

Combat Sustainment Support Battalions

C-7. Three to seven CSSBs may be assigned to a single sustainment brigade depending on the brigade's mission. The CSSB is under the C2 of the sustainment brigade commander. It is the base organization from which sustainment force packages are tailored for each operation. Through task organization, the CSSB is capable of providing sustainment support during all phases of operations. The CSSB is structured to optimize the use of sustainment resources (through SU and COP) and, therefore, minimize the amount of supplies and equipment in the AO. The mission of the CSSB is to C2 organic and attached units, provide training and readiness assistance, and provide sustainment technical advice, equipment recovery, and mobilization assistance to supported units. The headquarters detachment provides unit administration and logistic support to the battalion staff sections.

Ammunition Elements

C-8. Ammunition lift platoons or companies assigned to the CSSB operating an ASP provide for the receipt, storage, issue, and reconfiguration of ammunition items. These elements provide flexibility and can be tailored to support all types of operations ranging from high intensity major combat operations (MCO) to low intensity stability operations, to include transitions between types of operations. The modular-designed ammunition platoons can be attached as needed to meet surge requirements. Bulk class V is received by the TSC at the seaport of debarkation (SPOD). The ammunition element of the TSC configures class V within its ammunition storage activity (ASA). Then it is transported via throughput methods directly to using units or shipped to the tactical sustainment brigade ASA and to ammunition transfer and holding points (ATHP) for distribution to supported units as required.

Transportation Elements

C-9. Transportation elements of the CSSB provide mobility of personnel and all classes of supplies. When the CSSB is assigned to a sustainment brigade tasked to provide theater distribution capabilities, it will be heavily weighted with transportation assets. At the operational level, the CSSBs transportation assets will operate between the theater and the tactical sustainment brigade when loads cannot be throughput to the BSBs. At the tactical level, the CSSBs transportation assets will provide mobility from the CSSB base to the BSB.

Maintenance Elements

C-10. Maintenance assets of the CSSB provide maintenance based on the two-level (field and sustainment) maintenance concepts. At the field maintenance level, maintenance is focused on component replacement and rapid return of the repaired item to the user. Damaged but repairable components are then repaired by CSSB maintenance elements at the sustainment maintenance level. Repaired components are returned to the supply system. CSSB maintenance elements are designed with the capacity to send slice elements forward to support a maintenance surge or to help clear maintenance backlogs at the BSBs.

Supply and Services Element

C-11. Supply and services assets of the CSSB provide all classes of supplies and quality of life operations for personnel assigned or transiting the AO. Supply involves acquiring, managing, receiving, storing, and issuing all classes of supply. Field services involve feeding, clothing, and providing personnel services to Soldiers (clothing exchange, laundry and shower support, textile repair, mortuary affairs, preparation for aerial delivery, food services, billeting, and sanitation).

Movement Control Battalions

C-12. The movement control battalion (MCB) controls the movement of all personnel, units, and materiel in the assigned area of responsibility. It commands and controls between three and ten movement control teams. In the modular force, an MCB will be under the tactical control (TACON) or administrative control (ADCON) of a sustainment brigade operating in either the corps or numbered Army area of operations. The MCB is directly responsible and accountable to the TSC for the execution of the movement program and performance of the theater transportation system.

Other Agencies and Organizations

C-13. The sustainment brigade may be supported by a variety of other agencies and organizations. These will vary in both size and capability depending on the mission. They may require linkage into communications and data networks and must be considered in the planning and execution processes.

Theater Sustainment Command

C-14. When the sustainment brigade lacks the capacity to meet BCT logistics requirements, it coordinates with the TSC for required support. When the TSC receives the requirement, all resources in theater are options to meet the requirement. The TSC can cross-level between sustainment commands in theater or, using ITV, it can divert incoming cargo to meet demand. Requirements that cannot be met within the capability of the TSC are passed back to the CONUS logistics base.

Army Materiel Command Support

C-15. AMC support to deployed Army forces is executed through its AFSBs which, when fully operational, will be responsible to plan for and control all Army acquisition, technical logistic support, and technology (ALT) functions (less theater support contracting and LOGCAP), in the operational area.

C-16. The AFSB provides multiple capabilities in theater; it serves as the single point of contact for Army ALT support (less theater support contracting and LOGCAP) in the AO. Integrates and synchronizes ALT support to the ARMY FORCES operating in the AO. Providing command and control over subordinate AMC elements that provide direct support to tactical commanders. They also administer the Logistics Assistance Program (LAP) in the AO.

C-17. The AFSB is aligned to the ASCC in direct support to the senior sustainment commander (i.e. TSC/ESC) and maintains a technical relationship to AMC and applicable PEO/PM offices.

EAB Support for Medical and Class VIII

C-18. Army Health System support beyond the BCT BSMC capabilities are provided by EAB medical units. (See FM 4-02, FM 4-02.1, FM 4-02.12, and FM 4-02.21 for definitive information on EAB medical units and AHS operations.)

This page intentionally left blank.

Glossary

AHS	Army Health System
AIS	Automation Information Systems
ALOC	Administrative and Logistics Operation Center
AMC	Army Material Command
AMC/T	Aviation Maintenance Company/Troop
AO	Area of Operations
ASA	Ammunition Storage Activity
ASB	Aviation Support Battalion
ASC	Aviation Support Company
ASL	Authorized Stockage List
ATHP	Ammunition Transfer and Holding Point
AXP	Ambulance Exchange Point
BCS3	Battle Command Sustainment Support System
BCT	Brigade Combat Team
BDAR	Battle Damage Assessment and Repair
BFSB	Battlefield Surveillance Brigade
BMSO	Brigade Medical Supply Office
BSA	Brigade Support Area
BSB	Brigade Support Battalion
BSC	Brigade Support Company
BSMC	Brigade Support Medical Company
BSTB	Brigade Special Troops Battalion
CAB	Combat Aviation Brigade
CAISI	CSS Automation Information Systems Integrated
CBRN	Chemical, Biological, Radiological, and Nuclear
CEB	Clothing Exchange and Bath
CCI	Controlled Cryptographic Items
CFS	Call For Support
CK	Containerized Kitchen
COE	Combat Operating Environment
COEI	Components of End Items
COMSEC	Communications Security
COSC	Combat Operational Stress Control
CRT	Combat Repair Team
CSSB	Combat Sustainment Support Battalion
CTCP	Combat Trains Command Post
DCAM	Defense Customer Assistance Module
DMC	Distribution Management Center
DMLLS	Defense Medical Logistics Standard Support
DNBI	Disease Non-Battle Injury
DOS	Days of Supply
EAB	Echelons Above Brigade
EBS	Environment Baseline Survey
ECP	Enemy Control Points
EHSA	Environmental Health Site Assessment
ENCOORD	Engineer Coordinator
ESC	Expeditionary Sustainment Command
FDP	Forward Distribution Point
FM SPO	Financial Management Support Operations
FMC	Field Maintenance Company
FMT	Field Maintenance Team

FRAGO	Fragmentary Order
FSC	Forward Support Company
FST	Forward Surgical Team
GCSS-A	Global Combat Support System – Army
GSE	Ground Support Equipment
HBCT	Heavy Brigade Combat Team
HR	Human Resources
HSC	Headquarters and Support Company
IBCT	Infantry Brigade Combat Team
ICW	In Coordination With
IPB	Intelligence Preparation of the Battlefield
ITV	In -Transit Visibility
LAN	Local Area Network
LAP	Logistics Assistance Program
LOGCAP	Logistics Civil Augmentation Program
LOGSITREP	Logistics Situation Report
LRP	Logistics Release Point
LRU	Line Replicable Unit
LTO	Logistics Task Order
LWP	Lightweight Water Purifier
MA	Mortuary Affairs
MCB	Movement Control Battalion
MCO	Major Combat Operations
MCO	Movement Control Officer
MCP	Maintenance Collection Point
MCS	Maintenance Control Section
MCT	Movement Control Team
MDMP	Military Decision Making Process
MEB	Maneuver Enhancement Brigade
MEDSUP	Medical Supply
MI	Military Intelligence
MTF	Medical Treatment Facility
MTS	Movement Tracking System
NCS	Network Control Station
NICP	National Inventory Control Point
NMC	Non-Mission Capable
NRT	Near Real Time
NSC	Network Support Company
ODA	Special Forces Operations Detachment -Alpha
OP	Observation Posts
OPORD	Operations Order
QRF	Quick Reaction Force
PA	Physicians Assistant
PME	Peacetime Military Engagement
PMM	Preventative Medicine Measures
PT	Physical Therapy
PVNTMED	Preventive Medicine
ROM	Refuel on the Move
RP	Release Point
SASMO	Sustainment Automation Support Management Office
SBCT	Stryker Brigade Combat Team
SP	Start Point
SPO	Support Operations Officer
SPOD	Seaport of Debarkation
SSA	Supply Support Activity

STAMIS	Standard Army Management Information System
SU	Situational Understanding
TAMMS	The Army Maintenance Management System
TCF	Tactical Combat Forces
TSC	Theater Sustainment Command
TWPS	Tactical Water Purification System
UBL	Unit Basic Load
UMT	Unit Ministry Team
VSAT	Very Small Aperture Terminal

References

REQUIRED PUBLICATIONS

These documents must be available to intended users of this publication.

FM 1-02, Operational Terms and Graphics, 21 September 2004.
FM 3-0, Operations, 27 February 2008.
FM 3-90.6, The Brigade Combat Team, 4 August 2006.
FM 4-0, Sustainment, 30 April 2009.
FM 4-02.17, Preventive Medicine Services, 28 August 2000.
FM 8-250, Preventive Medicine Specialist, 27 January 1986.
FM 21-10, Field Hygiene and Sanitation, 21 June 2000.
FM 4-25.12, Unit Field Sanitation Team, 25 January 2002.
FM 4-02.1, Army Medical Logistics, 8 December 2009.
FM 4-02.21, Division and Brigade Surgeons' Handbook, Tactics, Techniques, and Procedures, 15 November 2000.
FM 1-0, Human Resources Support, 6 April 2010.
FM 4-02.51, Combat and Operational Stress Control, 6 July 2006.
FM 6-22.5, Combat and Operational Stress Control Manual for Leaders and Soldiers, 18 March 2009.
FM 4-02.12, Army Health System Command and Control Organizations, 27 July 2010.
FM 4-30.31, Recovery and Battle Damage Assessment and Repair, 19 September 2006.
AR 40-5, Preventive Medicine, 25 May 2007.

Joint Publications

Joint publications are available online: http://www.dtic mil/doctrine

JP 1-02, Department of Defense Dictionary of Military and Associated Terms, 12 April 2001.

RELATED PUBLICATIONS

These sources contain relevant supplemental information.

Army Publications

Army publications are available online at http://www.army mil/usapa/doctrine/active fm html
Army regulations and pamphlets are available online at http://www.army.mil/usapa/epubs/index html

AR 700-137, Logistics Civil Augmentation Program, 16 December 1985.
AR 710-2, Supply Policy Below the National Level, 28 March 2008.
AR 750-1, Army Materiel Maintenance Policy, 20 September 2007.
DA PAM 385-64, Ammunition and Explosives Safety Standards, 15 December 1999.
DA PAM 710-2-1, Using Unit Supply System (Manual Procedures), 31 December 1997.
DA PAM 750-8, The Army Maintenance Management System Users' Manual, 22 August 2005.
FM 3-04.111, Aviation Brigades, 7 December 2007.
FM 3-55.1, Battlefield Surveillance Brigade, 27 July 2010.
FM 3-90.31, Maneuver Enhancement Brigade Operations, 26 February 2009.
FM 4-02, Force Health Protection in a Global Environment, 13 February 2003.

FMI 4-93.2, The Sustainment Brigade, 4 February 2009.
FM 5-0, The Operations Process, 26 March 2010.
FM 6-0, Mission Command, Command and Control of Army Forces, 11 August 2003.
FM 55-30, Army Motor transportation Units and Operations, 27 June 1997.
FM 100-10.1, Theater Distribution, 1 October 1999.

Joint Publications

JP 4-01.4, Joint Tactics Techniques and Procedures for Joint Theater Distribution, 22 August 2000.

REFERENCED FORMS

DA Forms are available on the Army Publishing Directorate website (www.apd.army.mil).

DA FORM 2028, Recommended Changes to Publications and Blank Forms.
DA FORM 2406, Materiel Condition Status Report.

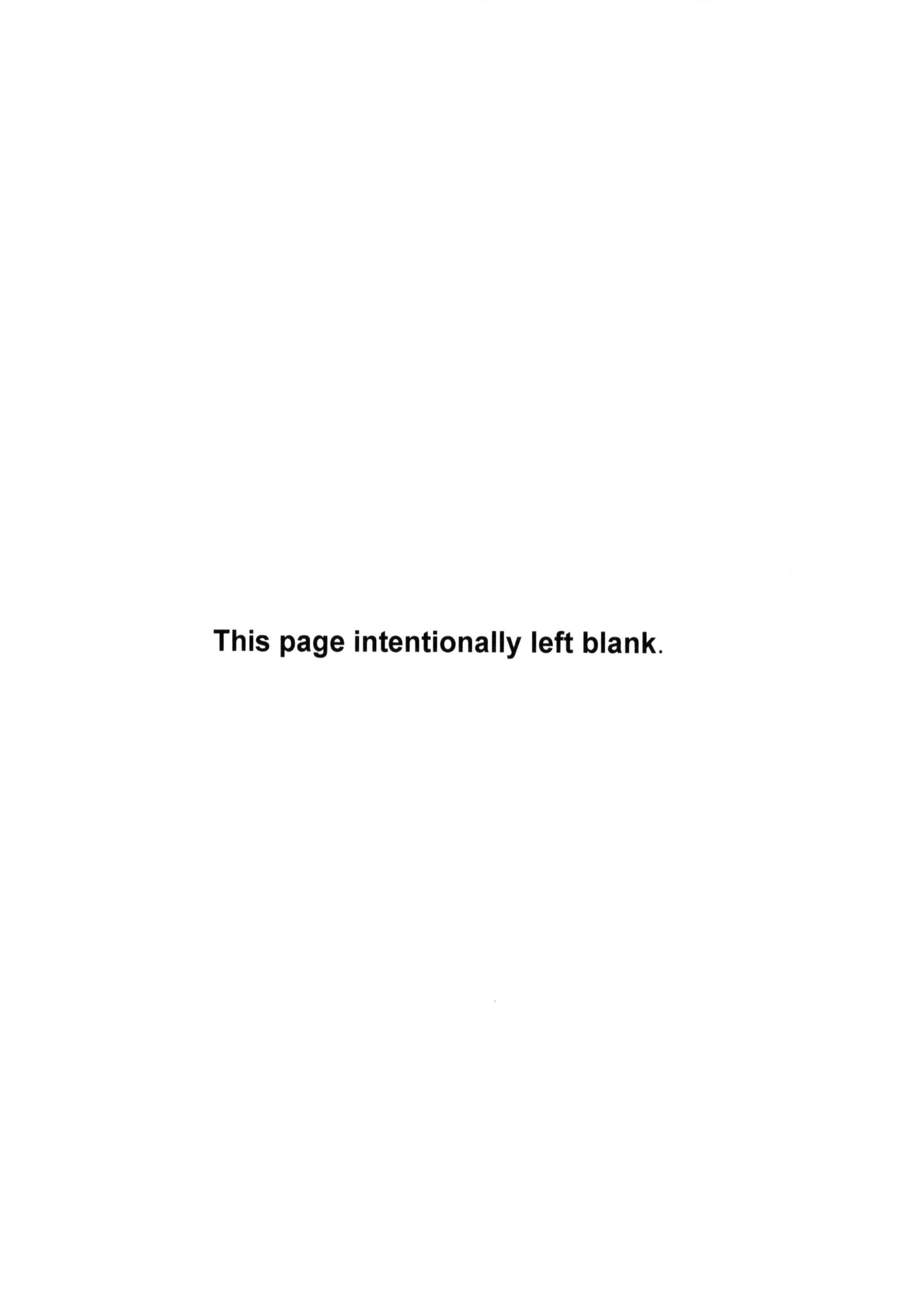

This page intentionally left blank.

Index

FM 4-90 (FM 4-90.7)
31 August 2010

By order of the Secretary of the Army:

GEORGE W. CASEY, JR.
General, United States Army
Chief of Staff

Official:

JOYCE E. MORROW
Administrative Assistant to the
Secretary of the Army
1022219

DISTRIBUTION:

Active Army, Army National Guard, and U.S. Army Reserve: Not to be distributed; electronic media only.

www.ingramcontent.com/pod-product-compliance
Ingram Content Group UK Ltd.
Pitfield, Milton Keynes, MK11 3LW, UK
UKHW051206260726
13967UKWH00011B/3136

9 781780 399447